MORE THAN MONEY

How Economic Inequality Affects EVERYTHING

Cover art by Paul Gill, designed by Paul Covello
Edited by Linda Pruessen
Copy-edited by Debbie Innis

Proofreader: Doeun Rivendell
Data Visualization Designer: Simone Betito

Interior designed by Maegan Fidelino

With special thanks to David Madani, Economist, for all the research and data he provided for this book.

The authors are grateful to Susan Traxel and the Office for National Statistics, U.K. Statistics Authority, for providing additional research and data; Linda Pruessen for her editorial guidance; Rivka Cranley and Paul Covello for their stewardship of the project, and the good people of Annick Press for their hard work, expertise, and patience.

Hadley Dyer extends additional thanks to Lena Coakley, Lucy Dyer, Marthe Jocelyn, Kathy Stinson, Emily van Beek, and Paula Wing for their support.

Mitchell Bernard thanks Jayne Edmonds for the feedback and the four-decade-long conversation.

Annick Press Ltd.

We acknowledge the support of the Canada Council for the Arts and the Ontario Arts Council, and the participation of the Government of Canada/la participation du gouvernement du Canada for our publishing activities.

Library and Archives Canada Cataloguing in Publication

Title: More than money : how economic inequality affects everything / Hadley Dyer and Mitchell
    Bernard ; illustrations by Paul Gill.
Names: Dyer, Hadley, author. | Bernard, Mitchell (Professor), author.
Identifiers: Canadiana (print) 20220170428 | Canadiana (ebook) 20220170487 | ISBN 9781773217017
    (softcover) | ISBN 9781773217000 (hardcover) | ISBN 9781773217048 (PDF) | ISBN 9781773217024
    (HTML)
Subjects: LCSH: Income distribution—Social aspects—Juvenile literature. | LCSH: Income distribution—
    Juvenile literature. | LCSH: Equality—Juvenile literature. | LCSH: Wealth—Social aspects—
    Juvenile literature. | LCSH: Quality of life—Juvenile literature.
Classification: LCC HC79.I5 D94 2022 | DDC j339.2/2—dc23

Published in the U.S.A. by Annick Press (U.S.) Ltd.
Distributed in Canada by University of Toronto Press.
Distributed in the U.S.A. by Publishers Group West.

Printed in Hong Kong

annickpress.com
hadleydyer.com
paullgill.com

Also available as an e-book. Please visit annickpress.com/ebooks for more details.

MORE THAN MONEY

How Economic Inequality Affects EVERYTHING

Written by Hadley Dyer and Mitchell Bernard

Illustrated by Paul Gill

annick press
toronto · berkeley

Table of Contents

PART ONE:
THE BASICS

PART TWO:
HAVE AND HAVE-NOTS

PART THREE:
TAKING ACTION

Introduction

What do you think of when you hear the word "inequality"?

If you're a math wizard, you might picture this: ≠. Or maybe your mind turns to social inequalities, such as racism (discrimination based on race) or sexism (discrimination based on gender).

Perhaps, to you, "inequality" is just another way of saying "unfairness."

You'd be right. Inequality can have multiple meanings, depending on the situation it's describing and whether it has another word in front of it.

This book is about economic inequality: why the rich are getting richer while everyone else seems to be struggling, more than ever, just to get by.

We know, we know—economics can be intimidating. It's full of confusing words. Charts and graphs. Statistics. *Math*. Ugh. Maybe you're not sure how economics is even relevant to your day-to-day life. But economics doesn't have to be scary or confusing, not if you have someone to break things down for you. That's what we're here to do.

For example, we'll explore why economic inequality isn't only about "the economy" but the kind of societies we live in.

We'll explain how it can have an impact on every aspect of your life, including your health, education, where you live, and how you feel about yourself.

You'll see how economic inequality is both a cause and an effect of different types of inequality.

We want you to understand how inequality affects everyone—rich, poor, and in-between. And we're going to show you what can be done about it.

By the end of this book, we'll have built a case for why economic inequality is a cause that you can rally behind with the same passion as climate change activists, gun control campaigns, and other youth-led movements.

Because inequality is really about YOUR future.

Researchers from the University of Wisconsin–Madison surveyed 600 students from middle schools and high schools in both richer and poorer communities. The students gave more concrete explanations for why people become rich— such as education, hard work, and inheriting money—than why people are poor.

OUR APPROACH

We'd like to acknowledge up front that this book is a primer, or overview, of a complex subject made up of connected issues, all of which are deserving of further attention. You'll find interesting—even startling—facts and statistics that may pique your curiosity and lead you to seek out more information. We raise questions to consider and discuss and provide additional resources throughout the book.

To get started, we'll walk you through the basic ideas and language that come up a lot in relation to inequality. Not every example will apply to your life right now (because maybe you don't have a rich portfolio of stocks and bonds?), but they'll help you get your head around important concepts.

We focus on economic inequality *within* a country: why some citizens are richer, and some are poorer. There's another type of economic equality, which is inequality *between* countries: why some countries are richer, and some are poorer. This is an important issue because it helps explain why the standards of living are so different for people around the world. But the causes of inequality between countries are complex and have long histories. We think that deserves its own book.

For our examples of inequality within countries, we stick with nations that are members of the **Organisation for Economic Co-operation and Development (OECD)**. The OECD is a Paris-based organization that collects and analyzes economic data provided by governments of thirty-eight countries. Most of the members have strong and stable economies and are among the world's richest countries. These include twenty-six European countries, plus North America, Chile, Colombia, Costa Rica, the United Kingdom, Israel, Japan, South Korea, Australia, and New Zealand.

There are a few reasons why we've chosen to focus on OECD countries. First, these are nations where all youth should face a bright future, but not everyone gets the same opportunities. Second, the majority of our readers live in OECD countries, which means they can relate to these examples. Lastly, the causes and solutions to inequality within less developed countries—countries with poorer and less stable economies—are somewhat different and complicated. We think comparing apples to apples is the easiest to understand.

Income Inequality in OECD Countries

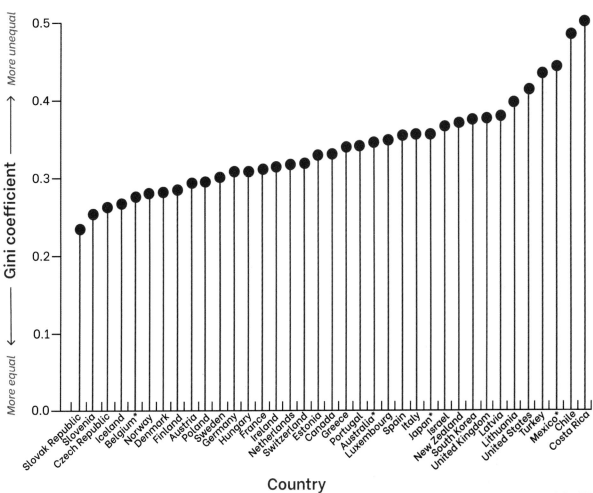

Source: OECD Statistics, 2017

This chart shows the level of inequality in each of the OECD countries, based on its Gini coefficient (see pages 22-23). The countries to the left of the chart are more equal, and those to the right are less equal. Once you've learned basic concepts about inequality in the first three chapters of this book, you can return to this chart whenever you need reminding of how each country ranks.

*Where 2017 scores were unavailable the most recent figures have been used.
*Colombia score not currently available from the OECD.

CHAPTER 1

Rich, Poor, and In-Between

Introduction:

WHAT IS INEQUALITY?

Throughout this book, we're going to meet characters and real people who are dealing with inequality in its various forms. To start, though, let's look back at something you experienced along with your family, friends, and millions of people around the world: the height of the COVID-19 pandemic.

Near the end of 2019, a highly contagious, potentially deadly virus called COVID-19, or the coronavirus, emerged in Wuhan, China. Transmitting from person to person, it rapidly made its way around the globe, forcing schools and workplaces to shut their doors in order to slow the spread of the disease.

From the beginning, the pandemic didn't affect everyone equally. Some people had a higher than average risk of becoming seriously ill or dying from the virus, which we'll take a closer look at in chapter 6. But the pandemic didn't just have an impact on health. For example, in many countries, schools carried on with classes through online learning, using video meetings, websites, and email to teach lessons. However, not all students could afford computers or tablets, or had access to Wi-Fi or parents at home to help them with their schoolwork. Students living in close quarters with their families struggled to find a quiet place to study. Kids who depended on school meal programs for breakfast or lunch faced the possibility of going hungry.

One definition of economic inequality is "the unequal distribution of income and wealth"—a stuffy way of saying that some people have more money and items of financial value than others. The COVID-19 pandemic showed us that inequality is about so much more than that. And while the pandemic affected young people and their families in vastly different ways, it didn't *create* inequality. Rather, it highlighted the inequality that was already there—and made it worse.

The first three chapters of this book will explore basic concepts related to "the unequal distribution of income and wealth." This chapter will focus on vocabulary and definitions that we'll keep returning to as you read on. But first, let us introduce what we call the "economic ladder"—and help you find your place on it.

THE ECONOMIC LADDER

Most of us would love to be rich, but ask five people what "rich" means and you might get five different answers.

Living in a nice house

Having an awesome
video game collection

Choosing clothes off the rack
without looking at the prices first

Being able to afford
any college or university

Retiring early

There are no official lines between "broke," "comfortable," and "loaded." Often, we judge our financial status by comparing ourselves to others. It's like being on a ladder, with people above you and below you.

Sometimes we might feel okay about our position . . .

. . . and sometimes, we might feel we've been left behind.

Economists rely on comparisons, using financial data to assess how well people are doing in relation to each other. Understanding these comparisons can help us see where we fit on the economic ladder. Are we at the top, where the air has that brand-new-Ferrari smell? Or closer to the bottom, struggling to get a foothold?

An economist studies the economy—the way money is made and how it is used within a geographical region, be that a country, state or province, or city.

FINDING YOUR RUNG

One way to find your place on the economic ladder
is through **income**—how much money you make.

The most common form of income is payment for work, such
as a salary or hourly wages. The more income you earn, the
higher your rung on the ladder.

To understand how differences in income lead to inequality,
it's helpful to first learn a little economics lingo.

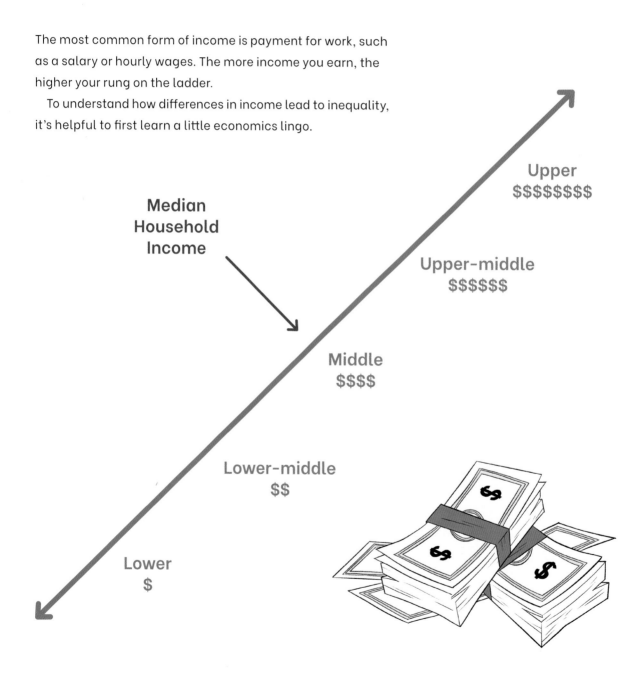

**Median
Household
Income**

Upper
$$$$$$$

Upper-middle
$$$$$$

Middle
$$$$

Lower-middle
$$

Lower
$

Economist-speak for the rungs on an income ladder is "**income distribution levels.**"

These levels are usually divided by **household income**, which is the total amount of money earned by all the people who share a home.

The **median** household income is a dollar amount that divides a population into two: half the households in that area earn more and half earn less.

The households closest to the median income are considered the **middle class**. As shown here, this category can be subdivided into *lower-middle*, *middle*, and *upper-middle*.

Exactly how much a household needs to earn in order to join each level depends on several factors, including where a family lives, what types of income are counted, and how many people share the home.

A typical chart or graph showing how income is distributed could have anywhere from three to one hundred levels. Here we use five. (The same goes for wealth, which we look at on page 12.)

GOING TO EXTREMES

There's rich and then there's *really* rich.

You may have heard top income earners referred to as **the one percent**. That's because they make more money than 99 percent of the rest of the population where they live. Within that one percent is the top **.01 percent**, who earn more than 99 percent of the one percent!

BELOW THE LINE

While everyone may have their own idea of what it means to be rich, we have a clearer definition for being poor. The **poverty line** is the minimum amount of income required to cover basic needs—including food, clothing, and shelter—for all the members of a household. Each country has its own poverty line that reflects the cost of living there and is used to determine if a household can receive financial help from government programs.

There is also a line for **extreme poverty**, which is based on the poverty lines of the world's poorest countries. A person who survives on less than $1.90 USD per day lives in extreme poverty and may be deprived of clean water, nutrition, health care, education, electricity, and sanitation.

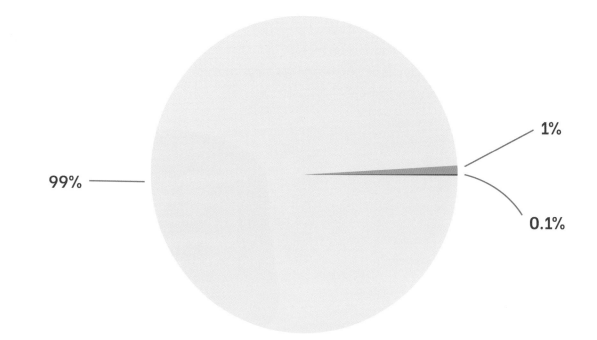

99% ——————

1%

0.1%

Pandemic Pay

The COVID-19 pandemic was both a health crisis and an economic crisis. The World Bank estimated that the pandemic pushed nearly 100 million people into extreme poverty. The most vulnerable were in developing countries, but people in richer countries suffered, too.

If your parents had well-paying office jobs, they may have been able to work from home while businesses were shut down to slow the spread of the virus. Lower-paid workers, such as store and restaurant staff, were far more likely to lose their jobs when their workplaces closed—temporarily or permanently. Many families started relying on food banks to stock their pantries.

OECD countries took different approaches to helping households that lost income during the pandemic. For example, several European governments covered most of the salaries for employees who held on to their jobs but couldn't go to work.

Some companies temporarily raised the wages of workers who were obliged to work during the pandemic despite the risks of becoming infected.

Young workers were among the most likely to become unemployed during the pandemic. In the U.K., nearly two-thirds of the workers who lost jobs during the early stages of the pandemic were under the age of twenty-five. In Canada, the government increased funding to its 2020 Canada Summer Jobs program to create up to 70,000 summer jobs for workers ages fifteen to thirty in the wake of the pandemic. It also temporarily paused repayments of student **loans** for six months and later suspended the accumulation of **interest** on student loans for two years.

MAKING BANK

So, a well-off person is someone who earns a high income. Seems simple enough—or is it?

What about the heiress who has never worked a day in her life thanks to an inheritance from her grandmother? Or the young professional who brings home a good paycheck but can't save any of it because he's paying off hefty student loans? Income alone doesn't offer a complete picture of a household's finances. We also have to look at wealth.

> "I made my money the old-fashioned way. I was very nice to a wealthy relative right before he died."
> —Malcolm Forbes, entrepreneur

ADDING IT UP

Wealth is all about what you're not spending day to day—your personal treasure chest. It could be money you've saved or inherited, as well as a variety of **assets**. These are items you could sell if you needed cash: a house, car, stocks, and other investments.

Your wealth is often measured as **net worth**: how much you'd have left over if you sold all your assets and paid all your debts.

PASSING IT ON

Wealth is accumulated over time and can be passed down from one generation to the next. It may stick around for a long time, especially for the one percent and the .01 percent. A study by the Bank of Italy revealed that many of the wealthiest families in Florence have been among the richest for almost 600 years!

HOW BIG IS YOUR TREASURE CHEST?

We can look at the wealth within a country by dividing its population into levels, as we do for income. The larger a household's net worth, the higher its level of wealth.

People who have lots of money left over after they pay their bills usually put it into **investments**: assets that may become more valuable over time, increasing the investor's wealth. These investments may include things like **stocks**, **bonds**, and real estate (not necessarily property they live on). If one investment fails, another may pick up the slack.

The biggest asset for most middle-class families is the home they own. When housing prices go up or down, so does the value of that asset, increasing or decreasing the net worth of its owners.

In bad economic times, the people hit hardest are those who live paycheck to paycheck, without any wealth to fall back on. These can be households from any income level—like that well-paid young professional we mentioned on the previous page, who has no money to spare because he's paying off student loans. But households with the lowest incomes are the most likely to have little to no wealth because every dollar goes toward covering their basic needs.

Investing in Investors

People tend to sell off their assets when the economy is doing poorly. In the early stages of the COVID-19 pandemic, the central banks—which manage a country's money supply and **monetary policies**—stepped in to stop this from happening. For example, in some countries, the central bank bought corporate bonds, which is a way of lending money to a company. This helped keep big companies going and encouraged **investors** not to sell off their own bonds and other assets. The luckiest ones even saw their net worth increase! But these actions did little to help people who depend on income, not investments, to stay afloat.

THE IN-BETWEENERS

What about you? Do you feel rich, poor, or in-between?

If you're American, chances are you believe you're in the middle level, or middle class. Surveys have shown that more than two-thirds of people in the United States think they're in the middle of the economic ladder. The reality is that only about half the population actually is middle class. The disconnect between reality and the way people perceive their financial level has been found in other countries, too.

Part of the confusion may be caused by how different middle-class lives look around the world. As discussed in the introduction to this book, inequality among countries means that your standard of living may depend on the place you call home. What's considered a low level of income or wealth in one country could be the middle level in another.

The homes on the facing page are typical of what a city-dwelling middle-class family could afford to buy in each country.

A VILLA IN MUMBAI

AN APARTMENT IN SHANGHAI

A VILLA IN BUENOS AIRES

A DETACHED HOME IN SYDNEY

The economic hardship caused by the COVID-19 pandemic showed how easy it is for middle-class families to slide down the economic ladder. Without a large treasure chest of savings to fall back on when their incomes dropped, many struggled to pay back the loans used to buy their homes, risking the loss of their biggest asset.

THE TAKEAWAY

The first step toward understanding inequality in a country or another geographical area is to compare the economic levels of the people who live there.

What Else We've Learned

 A household's economic level is determined by looking at both income and wealth.

 Having less wealth (or no wealth) as a safety net means lower-income families will suffer more when their incomes drop compared to families with more wealth.

The living standards of the middle class are different from one country to the next.

IDEAS IN ACTION

Italy was one of the worst-hit countries during the early days of COVID-19, but it also became the birthplace of a youth-led campaign to help those affected by the pandemic. Launched by teenager Nourhene Mahmoudi and other young volunteers, Outbreak of Generosity created a tool kit for youth across Europe that laid out how to support people in their communities who were lonely, isolated, or otherwise needed help during shutdowns and beyond. Translated into sixteen languages, the guide and campaign were supported by the Forum of European Muslim Youth and Student Organisations (FEMYSO), a community-action organization for youth that operates in twenty European countries.

LEARN MORE!

Outbreak of Generosity
outbreakofgenerosity.org

FEMYSO
femyso.org

DIGGING DEEPER

While the imagery of an economic ladder is useful, it might reinforce problematic ideas about income and wealth levels. Does a ladder suggest that the people on the higher rungs are more important? Does it imply that you should strive to get to the top, even though you can have a happy, comfortable life in the middle? What do you think? What imagery would you use to illustrate inequality instead?

CHAPTER 2

The Gap

Introduction:

HOW IS INEQUALITY MEASURED?

Meet Sophie from Oslo, Norway, and Michaela from London, England, in the United Kingdom. They both love soccer, K-pop, dogs, and mathematics. They both have annoying little brothers, and their families have lower-middle household incomes.

At first glance, their home countries have a lot in common, too. Norway and the U.K. are both in northern Europe. They have strong and stable economies. Most of their citizens enjoy a decent standard of living compared to people in poorer countries. But Norway is the fifth most equal country in the world, whereas the U.K. sits in thirty-second place.

The **income gap** grows when the earnings of those near the top of the income ladder increase at a faster rate than for those near the bottom. Similarly, the **wealth gap** grows when richer people increase their share of wealth compared to that of poorer people.

When discussing economic inequality, the media often focuses on income gaps, but wealth gaps tend to be bigger. In fact, the average wealth gap among OECD countries is about twice as big as the average income gap.

What does it mean for a country to be more or less equal? Let's go back to the economic ladder we talked about in chapter 1. Imagine how much income per year people might earn on the lower rungs of the ladder compared with those in the upper rungs. The bigger the gap between those amounts, the less equal the country. We can use wealth to judge how equal a country is by comparing the net worth of those on the top and bottom levels.

These gaps exist in every country in the world, but as we'll see in this chapter, some countries are more equal than others. We'll also look at how exactly equality is measured, why it's good to shrink economic gaps, and the difference shrinking the gaps can make in the lives of people like Sophie, Michaela, and their families.

JUST HOW (UN)EQUAL?

To get a clearer picture of economic gaps, let's trade the ladder for real numbers.

In this bar chart, we show household incomes in the United Kingdom.

As we did on page 8, we've divided the incomes into levels—ten levels this time, instead of five. Each bar represents the average income for households at that level. The higher the bar, the higher the income.

Check out the difference between the incomes for the top and bottom levels. The top earns nearly forty-two times more than the bottom!

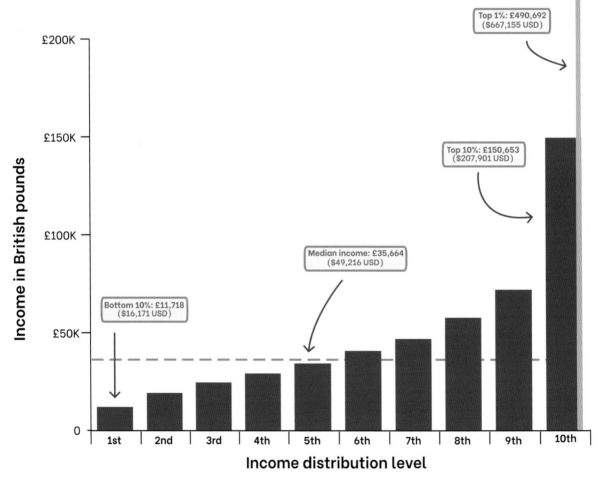

Top 1%: £490,692 ($667,155 USD)

Top 10%: £150,653 ($207,901 USD)

Median income: £35,664 ($49,216 USD)

Bottom 10%: £11,718 ($16,171 USD)

Income in British pounds

£200K
£150K
£100K
£50K
0

1st 2nd 3rd 4th 5th 6th 7th 8th 9th 10th

Income distribution level

Source: Office for National Statistics, 2020

Now let's look at wealth in the U.K. One way to do this is through a chart like the income chart on the facing page. We could simply swap income for wealth, again in British pounds. (You'll recall from page 12 that a household's wealth is based on the value of its assets—money in the bank, car, house, stocks, etc.)

But there's another way to study wealth. See that bar in the chart below that says "100% U.K. Wealth"? It represents the total amount of wealth owned by the entire population of the United Kingdom. It's like if everyone in the U.K. stashed their wealth in one big treasure chest.

How much a household adds to the treasure chest depends on how wealthy it is. The other bars in the chart show what percentage of the U.K.'s wealth is owned by the households at each level. This percentage is known as each group's **share of wealth.**

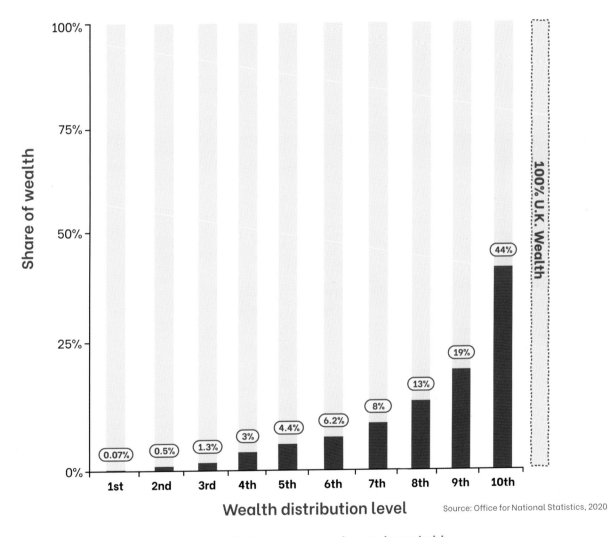

Source: Office for National Statistics, 2020

The richest households' share of wealth is 44 percent, whereas households at the bottom level own just .07 percent of the country's total wealth.

INEQUALITY AROUND THE WORLD

You might be surprised to discover which countries are more equal and which are less. Countries that have similar cultures or share borders may have different-sized gaps in income or wealth among their citizens.

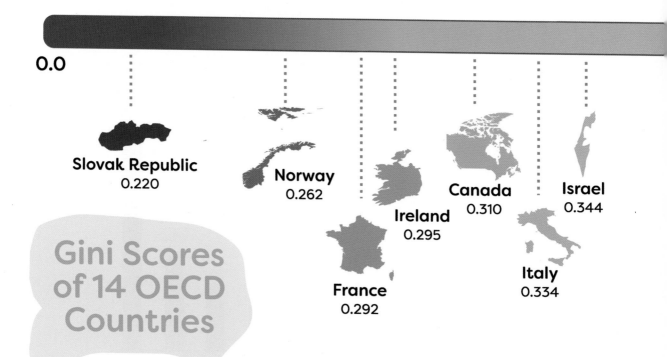

0.0

Slovak Republic
0.220

Norway
0.262

Ireland
0.295

Canada
0.310

Israel
0.344

France
0.292

Italy
0.334

Gini Scores of 14 OECD Countries

Source: OECD Statistics, 2017

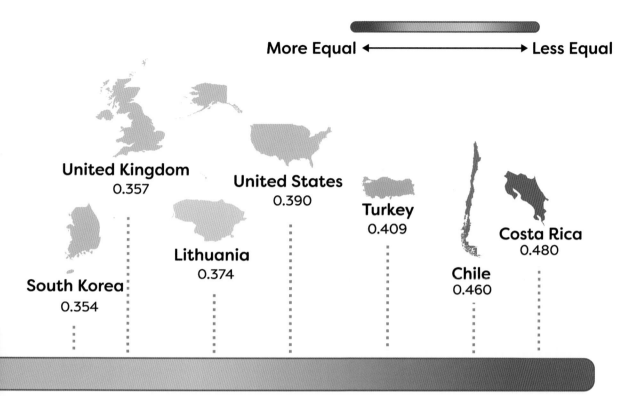

United Kingdom
0.357

United States
0.390

Turkey
0.409

Costa Rica
0.480

Lithuania
0.374

South Korea
0.354

Chile
0.460

0.5

Ask the Gini

Economists compare inequality around the world in a variety of ways, each painting its own picture depending on the method, the type of data used, and the data's source. Many international organizations, including the United Nations and World Bank, use a method called the **Gini coefficient**, or Gini index. It represents the amount of income or wealth equality in a country as a number between zero and one. A score of zero would mean a country is perfectly equal because everyone earns the same amount of income or has the same share of wealth. A score of one would mean a country is perfectly unequal because just one household earns all the income or owns all the wealth.

WHY SHRINK THE GAPS?

There's an ongoing debate among economists and politicians about whether governments should be more concerned with closing income and wealth gaps or just raising people out of poverty.

Who cares how much people have at the top as long as there are fewer people at the bottom, right? Besides, we can't all be rich.

It may be true that there's no perfectly equal country, let alone one where everyone is loaded. It's also true, though, that almost everyone is better off when a society is more equal and has a strong, stable middle class. Here are just a few of the reasons, which we'll be exploring in more detail in later chapters.

HEALTHIER

In OECD countries, there aren't clear links between health problems and the country's average income. However, there are links between health problems and income *gaps*. More-equal countries tend to invest in things that safeguard their citizens' health, such as health care and pollution control, which can lead to longer, healthier lives. They also have fewer heart-related hospitalizations and deaths, and fewer infant deaths than less equal countries.

The U.K. has more than double the obesity rate of Norway.

SAFER

Research has shown that places with a larger gap between rich and poor have higher crime rates. These aren't just economic crimes. There is a strong correlation between inequality and violent crime, including homicides.

According to the OECD, these countries rank among the ten least equal *and* the ten least safe among its members: Chile, Latvia, Lithuania, Mexico, Turkey.

These member countries are among the ten most equal and the ten safest: Austria, Denmark, Finland, Iceland, Norway, and Slovenia.

MORE DEMOCRATIC

Rich people have the **resources** to pressure politicians through political campaign contributions and lobbying. (To learn about lobbying, check out chapter 7.) Some own media corporations, which allows them to influence which issues get covered and how they are presented. But when the middle class is large and holding steady, politicians have to listen to its concerns, too.

MORE PROSPEROUS

Middle-class families use their **disposable income**—money left over after covering basic expenses—to purchase all kinds of goods and services, from electronics to gym memberships to restaurant meals. Poorer families have less disposable income, and while richer families have more, they tend to save or invest a great deal of it. When the middle class shrinks, so does its spending power, which hurts the economy. That affects everyone, even the one percent.

Research shows that people feel like they have a greater stake in their political system when they believe it to be fair.

The poverty rate in Norway is 8 percent versus 12 percent in the U.K.

MORE VERSUS LESS

One of the most obvious ways a more equal country may improve life for its citizens is simply making important things more affordable.

This can help boost lower-income families up the economic ladder, including those we met at the beginning of this chapter—Sophie's in Oslo, Norway, and Michaela's in London, England (U.K.).

Paid parental leave for one or both parents gives mothers time to heal after giving birth, and parents a chance to bond with their child without suffering financial hardship.

When Sophie's little brother was born, her parents took forty-nine weeks of paid parental leave between them. When Michaela's brother was born, her parents were able to take off fifty weeks between them, but only thirty-seven were paid.

Subsidized childcare reduces one of the most expensive costs for families.

Sophie's parents spend less money on services that are covered by **benefits**—government programs that offer financial support to citizens. One of these benefits is childcare, which is much less expensive in Norway compared to the U.K. That makes it easier for both of Sophie's parents to go to work and earn income for their family. About one-third of Norway's budget goes to these kinds of benefits.

Well-funded schools are more likely to have programs for students with special needs, from support for learning difficulties to language training for immigrants.

Free or low-cost universities, colleges, and vocational (job) training schools remove barriers to higher learning and better jobs.

In the U.K., educational achievement is more connected to income: richer kids have a better chance of getting a higher level of education than poorer kids. In Norway, public universities are tuition-free, so students from all income levels can attend. (Public programs are those that get funding from government.)

Government-supported extracurricular activities, such as sports, keep kids healthy, create social connections, and build life skills.

Richer children in the U.K. get more physical activity than poorer children. They can also afford to eat more fresh fruit and vegetables, which lowers their risk for obesity and other health issues. In Norway, government programs help make athletics and nutritious food more accessible.

HOW NORWAY PAYS FOR IT

Taxes on a wide range of goods and services help make Norway one of the most expensive countries to live in. However, the taxes collected by the Norwegian government pay for benefits like those we've just listed. Taxes are lower in the U.K., but families like Michaela's may pay more for similar services, leaving them with less income to spare. Additionally, salaries are higher in Norway than in the U.K., which means Sophie's parents make more money to pay for things the government doesn't help out with. We take a deeper dive into how taxes can address inequality in chapter 7.

THE TAKEAWAY

Though Sophie's and Michaela's families live in the same region of Europe and have similar household incomes, Sophie's family may enjoy a better quality of life.

What Else We've Learned

 The bigger the economic gaps between rich and poor, the less equal a country.

 Countries that seem similar on the surface may not have the same level of economic equality.

 More-equal societies are often safer, healthier, more prosperous, and more democratic.

 Common expenses like childcare and education are made more affordable in more-equal countries.

IDEAS IN ACTION

More than 90 percent of Norwegian children play organized sports, thanks to a government policy called "Children's Rights in Sport," which guarantees every child the opportunity to participate in athletic activities.

In Finland, daycare centers provide child-care for working parents and early education for children. Fees are scaled according to the family's income and number of children, with the government covering the entire fee for the lowest-income families.

Germany offers free university tuition to all European and international students. The most expensive OECD countries for post-secondary education include the United States, the United Kingdom, and Luxembourg.

LEARN MORE!

The Norwegian Olympic and Paralympic Committee and Confederation of Sports (NIF)
idrettsforbundet.no

CONSIDER THIS

"One of the reasons inequality gets so deep in this country is that everyone wants to be rich. That's the American ideal. Poor people don't like talking about poverty because even though they might live in the projects surrounded by other poor people and have, like, ten dollars in the bank they don't like to think of themselves as poor." —JAY-Z, recording artist

CHAPTER 3

Moving Up

Introduction:

CLIMBING THE LADDER

Isaiah's parents moved to the United States shortly after he was born. They secured lower-income jobs for themselves and hoped to give their son a brighter future in a more prosperous country. With hard work, a bit of luck, and a lot of heart, any American can transform their lives, or so the story goes.

MEET ISAIAH FROM BOSTON, MASSACHUSETTS.

Son of hardworking immigrants from Haiti.
Future software developer.
Sneaker addict.

This change in fortunes from poorer to richer is known as **upward mobility**, and many immigrants arrive in the United States with the same aspirations. In his 1931 bestseller *The Epic of America*, author James Truslow Adams described the American Dream as "that dream of a land in which life should be better and richer and fuller for everyone, with opportunity for each according to ability or achievement."

Yet, the chances of going from low income to middle income are worse in the United States than in most OECD countries. When poorer people have a harder time moving up the economic ladder, income and wealth gaps can grow.

In this chapter, we'll look at the different types of upward mobility and data that shows which countries have the most upward mobility, and learn why the best chance at achieving your goals might be trading the American Dream for a Nordic one.

TYPES OF UPWARD MOBILITY

Social and economic mobility can go upward or downward, and there are multiple ways to measure it. To illustrate this, let's fast-forward to a future where Isaiah has achieved his dream of becoming a well-paid software developer by age 28.

Intragenerational mobility measures changes to a person's economic or social status during their lifetime.

The mobility is absolute if a person is in a higher or lower economic distribution level compared to where they started.

 Isaiah's income: $68,000
Median income in Boston, Massachusetts: $65,883

Isaiah grew up in a low-income household, but his current income level is considered middle class where he lives.

The mobility is relative if a person is better or worse off in comparison with *other people* who entered the workforce around the same time.

Isaiah's income: $68,000
Median income for 18- to 34-year-olds in Boston: $45,000

Isaiah is doing better financially than other workers his age.

Intergenerational mobility measures differences in the economic or social status of two generations of the same family.

The mobility is absolute if a person is better or worse off than their parents when making a direct comparison between their incomes or net worth.

 Isaiah's parents' total household income: $43,000

Isaiah's income: $68,000

 Isaiah's salary is 58 percent higher than his parents' incomes combined.

Isaiah's parents. Dry cleaner and part-time store clerk.

Best **DRY CLEANING** In Town!

The mobility is relative if a person ends up in a different income or wealth distribution level than their parents.

 Isaiah's parents: Low-income level
Isaiah: Middle-income level

Upward mobility isn't about getting rich or buying more sneakers. The higher Isaiah moves within the middle class, the less danger there is that he will quickly tumble out of it if he has a change in fortune, like losing his job.

THE AMERICAN DREAM

In the future, Isaiah will experience every type
of upward mobility and make his parents proud.

What his story doesn't tell us is how he beat
the odds. In the United States, only one in ten
people born into low-income families will make
it to the upper-income level, and about a third
won't budge from where they started. The
data is clear: it can be tough for kids born into
lower-income families to move up the economic
ladder in the United States. But that's not true
everywhere.

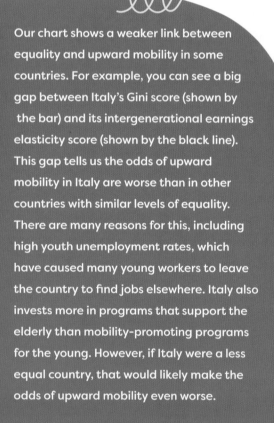

Our chart shows a weaker link between
equality and upward mobility in some
countries. For example, you can see a big
gap between Italy's Gini score (shown by
the bar) and its intergenerational earnings
elasticity score (shown by the black line).
This gap tells us the odds of upward
mobility in Italy are worse than in other
countries with similar levels of equality.
There are many reasons for this, including
high youth unemployment rates, which
have caused many young workers to leave
the country to find jobs elsewhere. Italy also
invests more in programs that support the
elderly than mobility-promoting programs
for the young. However, if Italy were a less
equal country, that would likely make the
odds of upward mobility even worse.

DREAM OR ILLUSION?

On the facing page is a type of chart known
as the "Great Gatsby Curve." It was named for
F. Scott Fitzgerald's classic novel about the
illusion of the American Dream because it shows
that upward mobility is less likely in the U.S.
compared to other rich countries.

Our Great Gatsby Curve compares how equal
a country is to its intergenerational mobility—
whether a child's income will be better than their
parents' once they've grown up.

The bars on the chart represent the level of
equality in a country, measured by its Gini score.
As we learned on page 23, the closer to zero, the
more equal the country. This means the more
equal countries are those with the lower bars on
the right, and the less equal countries have the
higher bars on the left.

The line running across the chart has an
intimidating label: intergenerational income
elasticity. This is a way of measuring how likely
it is that someone will end up at the same income
level as their parents. Like the Gini coefficient,
it's a score of zero to one. A score of zero means
there's no connection between a grown child's
income and their parents'. A score of one
means they'll end up at the exact same level
as their parents.

For upward mobility, the less your parents' economic status matters, the better. So, as with the Gini score: less is more.

What do we see? With the exception of those spikes over Italy and France, the line follows the height of the bars as it slopes downward toward more equality. The bottom line (no pun intended) is that the more equal the country, the less your parents' income matters when it comes to your future.

> "If you want the American Dream, go to Finland."
>
> —Ed Miliband, British Member of Parliament

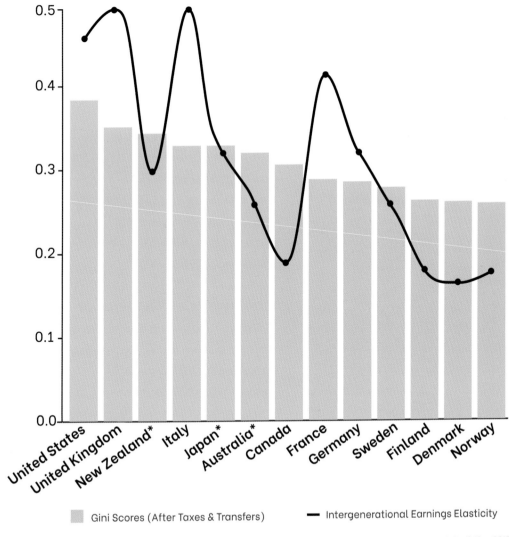

Gini Scores (After Taxes & Transfers)   ▬ Intergenerational Earnings Elasticity

Source: OECD Statistics, 2017; Miles Corak, 2012

*Where 2017 scores were unavailable, the most recent figures have been used.

THE REPORT CURVE

As we've seen, the gaps between rich and poor really matter.
It also matters whether a gap is growing or shrinking.
Who is moving up, moving down, or staying still?

We've got one final chart for you. This one shows how incomes have changed around the globe over the past four decades. Where have incomes gotten better? Where have they gotten worse? Who has earned a passing grade on improving equality?

Along the bottom of the graph, the world's population has been divided into groups of equal size. The group with the lowest income level is on the far left. As you move right, the income levels rise.

Along the side of the graph, we see how much the average income rose or fell between 1980 and 2016.

STEADY PROGRESS

To the far left of the graph, we see that incomes rose for the world's lowest income earners, which means fewer people live in extreme poverty compared to forty years ago. That seems like a good thing. However, when we dig into the data behind the graph, we find out that most of these gains were made in China, the world's most populous country, not equally across less developed countries.

ROOM FOR IMPROVEMENT

As we move toward the right side of the chart, we can see more people moving up to join the middle class within their countries. But these incomes are still relatively low, well below the standard of living for the middle class in most OECD countries.

STRUGGLING TO KEEP UP

The income levels from 50 to 90 include lower-middle and middle-income earners in North America and Western Europe. The fairly straight line across the curve tells us that incomes have grown little to none in this range since 1980.

DOES NOT PLAY WELL WITH OTHERS

To the far right of the graph, the line curves steeply upward, along with incomes for the top one percent (and up), which have grown almost twice as much as those in the bottom 50 percent, especially in rich, less equal countries.

Even though incomes have improved for many of the world's poorest people, the curve shows that the income gap between rich and poor is now bigger than ever.

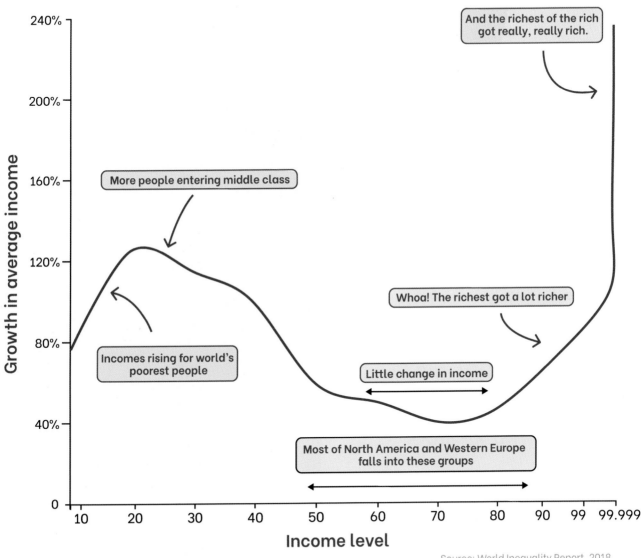

Growth in average income (y-axis)

240%
200%
160%
120%
80%
40%
0

Income level (x-axis)

10   20   30   40   50   60   70   80   90   99   99.999

And the richest of the rich got really, really rich.

More people entering middle class

Whoa! The richest got a lot richer

Incomes rising for world's poorest people

Little change in income

Most of North America and Western Europe falls into these groups

Source: World Inequality Report, 2018

Source: World Inequality Database, Working Papers Series, N° 2017/20

THE TAKEAWAY

One of the greatest predictors of upward mobility is the country where you were born. Though you *can* achieve upward mobility in a less equal country, you have a better chance of moving up the economic ladder in a more equal country.

What Else We've Learned

 There are multiple types of upward mobility, and a person can achieve some or all of them.

 The American Dream may be harder to achieve in the United States than in other OECD countries.

Incomes have improved for many of the world's poorest people, but overall the gap between rich and poor is growing.

IDEAS IN ACTION

If you want to get ahead in life, you need to put your head down and work as hard as possible—that's the kind of advice teens hear a lot, especially as they get closer to graduation. But even in more-equal countries, where the odds of upward mobility are better for everyone, the pressure to perform can take a toll. After suffering a panic attack at her school in Sherwood, Oregon, Hailey Hardcastle called her mom and asked if she could come home. Then eighteen, she was suffering from the stress of schoolwork and preparing college applications on top of an anxiety disorder and episodes of depression. What she needed more than anything was a day off. Taking the time to rest helped Hailey rebound and reclaim her mental health—and she began a campaign advocating for all students in Oregon to have the opportunity to do the same. Just a year later, the state legislature passed a law mandating that all students be entitled to mental health days, a law that Hailey herself helped to write.

THE PLAYLIST

"A Beautiful Chicago Kid"—Common

"All the Above"—Maino

"The Climb"—Miley Cyrus

"Fast Car"—Tracy Chapman

"Living for the City"—Stevie Wonder

"Lose Yourself"—Eminem

"Work B**ch"—Britney Spears

LEARN MORE!

Hailey Hardcastle
@hailey.hardcastle

Hailey's TED Talk:
"Why Students Should Have Mental Health Days"
ted.com/talks/hailey_ hardcastle_the_case_for_ student_mental_health_days/ transcript

The World Inequality Database
wid.world

DIGGING DEEPER

Throughout this book, we share statistics that demonstrate the sad fact that a person's economic status can create extra challenges for them in life, especially in less equal places. Some readers may find this data reassuring because it acknowledges these hurdles are real. It also counteracts the myth that poorer people simply don't work hard enough or dream big enough. But while statistics do not determine the future, what if they create the *perception* that your fate is already set? What kind of language should we use when discussing these kinds of statistics to ensure they do not create a sense of hopelessness?

PART TWO

Have and Have-Nots

CHAPTER 4

A Growing Problem

Introduction:

THE NATURAL ORDER

Pope Francis took his papal name in honor of Saint Francis of Assisi, an Italian friar and deacon born around 1181 who became the patron saint of Italy, animals, and nature.

In his teenage years, Francesco—as Saint Francis was called at the time—was the epitome of privilege: a rich, lazy, guitar-playing party boy who dropped out of his studies to devote more time to drinking and carousing. He eventually served in the military, which led to a year as a prisoner of war, followed by a serious illness and a radical change of heart. He cast off his wealth, took a vow of poverty, and devoted his life to the poor and the teachings of the church.

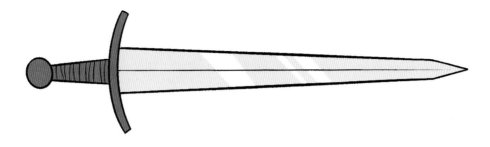

Saint Francis of Assisi's renunciation of his wealth was as exceptional then as it would be today. Throughout much of history, your life's path was pretty much fixed at birth. In Medieval Europe, for example, it was said that you were born to work (peasants), born to pray (the clergy), or born to fight (warriors). If your father was a farmer, chances were you would be, too—for life.

When you consider the long history of princes and peasants, it's easy to assume we've always been this way, that Assisi picked a fight with the natural of things. Humans must be instinctively competitive and obsessed with who's on top.

Or are we?

In this chapter, we go back in time to the origins of economic inequality. We'll take a look at the more-equal ways of our ancient ancestors and theories about how inequality grew over time. We'll then examine three developments that have further increased inequality in a number of OECD countries over the past few decades. These developments have made upward mobility difficult for many—and downward mobility a real possibility for some. But history also reveals that just because inequality has been getting worse doesn't mean it's natural or unavoidable.

> "We go our way in haste, without worrying that gaps are increasing, that the greed of a few is adding to the poverty of many others."
>
> —Pope Francis, head of the Catholic Church, 2019

HAVE HUMANS ALWAYS BEEN UNEQUAL?

For the tens of thousands of years before there were grocery stores or even farms, people survived by hunting animals and gathering plants.

The few remaining hunter-gatherer societies may offer clues to how our earliest ancestors lived. Genetic testing of the Hadza, an Indigenous people living in northern Tanzania, shows their DNA lineage dates back more than 100,000 years. The fossil record suggests that people throughout East Africa used to hunt, gather, and live in groups much like the Hadza do today. Out of a population of 1,000 to 1,500 individuals, about a quarter of the Hadza still rely exclusively on hunting and gathering to sustain themselves.

Like most surviving hunter-gatherer societies, the Hadza are **egalitarian**, which means that everyone is considered equal. They live in groups of twenty to forty people who share food, water, weapons, tools, and land. Most of the "wealth" that is passed on through generations takes the form of advantages like health, hunting skills, and strong relationships.

Egalitarian societies aren't just economically equal but also socially equal. No one person or group has power or authority over others. Individuals are free to make decisions for themselves as long as they don't hurt the group.

We don't know for certain if our earliest ancestors were as equal as the Hadza, but egalitarian hunter-gatherer societies do show that inequality is *not* inevitable.

You Call That Lunch?

The Ju/'hoansi people of the Kalahari Desert in southern Africa have a trick for keeping egos in check so they don't threaten the equality within their society. When hunters return home with fresh game, the meat is insulted instead of praised. As a Ju/'hoans man explained to Canadian anthropologist Richard B. Lee: "When a young man kills much meat, he comes to think of himself as a chief or big man—and thinks of the rest of us as his servants or inferiors. We can't accept this . . . so we always speak of his meat as worthless. This way, we cool his heart and make him gentle."

THE BEGINNING OF RICH AND POOR

So, if inequality isn't inevitable, how did we become so unequal?

Many anthropologists believe that the arrival of **agriculture**—growing crops, raising live-stock—about 12,000 years ago played a big part. Growing and raising our food changed how we eat, work, and live together.

KA-CHING!

Before the invention of money, people traded goods and labor. Over time, items such as salt, furs, seeds, and weapons became preferred trading items because they were both valuable and easy to exchange. The first minted coin currency was introduced in 600 BCE, followed by the first bank notes (bills) in 1661 CE. By the Middle Ages, "money" was borrowed and lent for spending, investing, and trading.

MORE THAN ENOUGH

For the first few thousand years of agriculture, our ancestors produced just enough food to feed their families—known as **subsistence farming**—and continued to hunt and gather. As they grew more grains, they started producing surplus crops. Grains could be stored for long periods and traded for other things. They could also create debts between those who produced too little and those who produced too much. In some societies, families began to take ownership over the land they cultivated, passing it from one generation to the next. Control of surpluses and land were early forms of wealth, and over time, the distribution of that wealth became very unequal.

RISE OF THE STATE

As agriculture developed, people began settling into villages of 100 to 200 inhabitants. About 6,000 years ago, some of those villages expanded into cities of thousands. Farming increased in scale with larger crops to feed growing populations, and the first states emerged.

A **state** is a territory that is organized under a leadership, such as a monarchy or another form of government. In order to thrive, a state needs things like roads to connect its different parts, irrigation systems to deliver water to people and crops, and an army to protect its land from rival states. These resources and services, which benefit all or most members of a state, are known as **public goods**. To create public goods, states started collecting taxes, which in their earliest incarnation may have been a share of crops or working on behalf of the state.

New jobs appeared: tax collectors, managers, servants, priests, and soldiers. A large workforce was required to tend the fields, which led to those in power forcing others into labor, including slavery. In their quest for evermore wealth, humans had begun dividing societies into "haves" and "have-nots."

Crib Size

Archaeologists from Washington State University and Arizona State University measured the sizes of ancient house ruins on sixty-three archaeological sites in Europe, Asia, North America, and Central America. Dating as far back as 9000 BCE, these were the former living sites of hunter-gatherers, villages with small farms, and early Roman cities. They theorized that richer families had bigger dwellings—and so the larger the differences in house sizes at a given site, the less equal that society may have been. Based on these comparisons, they concluded that inequality arrived with agriculture and increased over time, though there were a few societies that remained relatively equal long after they began farming on a large scale.

HOW WORK HAS CHANGED

One reason for growing inequality over the past few decades is that how we work is continuously changing.

As societies developed, so did the special skills of their workforce, leading to a new class of craftspeople and artists.

Land became a **commodity**—something that could be bought, sold, and used in different ways to make a profit. Landowners became landlords while tenant farmers did the hard labor or . . .

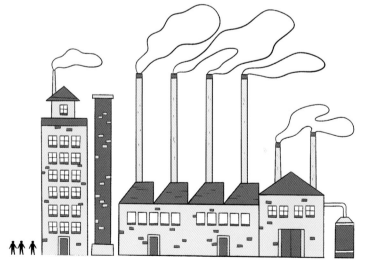

. . . left farming to work in the trades. Starting in the late eighteenth century, the technological advances of the Industrial Revolution allowed factories to make products on a massive scale.

Millions of factory laborers worked long hours, often under unsafe conditions for little pay.

During the "Gilded Age" before the outbreak of World War I, and after the war, economic gaps grew. Rich people on both sides of the Atlantic flaunted their wealth and free time while the average worker struggled to get by.

After World War II . . . a manufacturing BOOM! Many countries saw major economic growth and the expansion of industries, including automobiles, electronics, and aviation.

In 1913, American industrialist Henry Ford set in motion the first assembly line, allowing factories to mass produce automobiles under one roof in a fraction of the time it used to take.

Wages became high enough for workers in industries like manufacturing to join the middle class. More people were employed in "white-collar" jobs*, including teachers, engineers, and managers.

It was a brave new world!
So many people were optimistic about the future. That is, until . . .

*To learn about the origins of the term "white-collar," see page 115.

ATTACK OF THE ROBOTS!!!

Every era has brought new technological advances that have eliminated jobs once performed by people.

Switchboard operators were replaced with modern telephones. Town criers were replaced by mass-produced newspapers and then radio, television, and the Internet. Streetlamps now light themselves automatically when darkness falls. More recently, stores have introduced self-checkout so that customers no longer need a clerk to assist them. Soon, we may see self-driving vehicles replacing transit, taxi, and truck drivers.

This process of trading people for machines and other technology is known as **automation**, and it has had a profound impact on industries that used to employ large numbers of middle-class workers. The United States is manufacturing more than ever, but the number of American assembly-line workers has dropped dramatically. The loss of these jobs has made it harder than

ever for many people to move up—or hold on to their place on—the economic ladder.

WHAT'S NEXT?

Automation has had the biggest impact on jobs that don't require years of higher education or training. As technology becomes more sophisticated, artificial intelligence may start replacing jobs that require more schooling too.

For example, financial advisors may find themselves in competition with cutting-edge software that can advise people on how to invest their money. You might ask: Why work hard and stay in school if a robot army is going to replace us all?

Because it isn't. In a lot of professions, humans beat robots every time.

These are often jobs that require person-to-person interactions, such as law, health care, childcare, and support for the elderly. They include jobs in the arts, design, cooking, and craftwork, as well as in technology, which will always need people to invent, repair, and advance it. In fact, experts say that instead of training for lifelong careers, young people today should focus on lifelong learning, developing skills that can be useful in multiple fields: empathy, analysis, communications, critical thinking, numeracy, and creativity.

A **profit** is the amount of money made from selling a product or service after costs are subtracted. During the economic boom following World War II, workers' wages tended to go up as companies increased their profits. In recent decades, developments like increased automation have led to wages going down even when profits go up.

As manufacturing jobs have dried up, many workers have moved into jobs in the service industry. Unfortunately, in some countries, service-industry wages have been sliding over the past few decades. We explore why on pages 94–95.

And let's not forget that technology has also created whole industries and jobs that didn't exist before—from pilots and computer programmers to special-effects designers, lab technicians, and social media influencers. Our modern world has no shortage of problems to be solved with the help of technology, one of the biggest of which is climate change. How many jobs could be created through the production of more renewable energy, retrofitting buildings to save energy, and new methods of recycling waste?

GOING GLOBAL

Automation wasn't the only development of the past four decades that struck a blow against the middle class and upward mobility, especially among workers in the manufacturing industry.

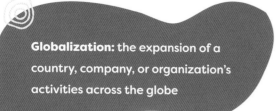

Globalization: the expansion of a country, company, or organization's activities across the globe

Lower wages in Asia have allowed manufacturers to charge less for their products while making bigger profits—good news for shoppers looking for cheaper prices, bad news for the workers whose jobs have been sent overseas.

These developing industries have also lifted millions of Asian workers out of poverty, though it should be noted that many labor under unfair and unsafe working conditions.

Starting in the 1960s, companies in North America and Europe (and, later, Japan) began sending the parts for their products to Asia, where the workforces of Hong Kong, Taiwan, and others in the region assemble products for relatively low wages. The finished items are then imported to the company's home country or exported to other international markets.

Through the 1970s and 1980s, more Asian countries became assembly hubs, including Thailand, Malaysia, and Indonesia. In the 2000s, China emerged as an assembly-line superpower in the production of textiles, clothing, electronic components, and consumer electronics. It was soon producing and assembling virtually all household items, from furniture to light bulbs to toys.

Heavier products are expensive to ship, so some industries, like the auto industry, began assembling their products closer to home. For example, a number of American automakers assemble their vehicles in Mexico.

HOW A SMARTPHONE GETS MADE

Meet the hottest new smartphone on the market: the mePhone! Let's follow its journey around the globe from invention to delivery into your eager hands.

A patent is the legal right to exclusively make, use, and sell an invention. Like most of the patents for smartphone technology, the patents for the mePhone are owned by American companies based in California, where the device is designed and tested.

One of the minerals needed to make the mePhone is cobalt, which is used for the phone's rechargeable lithium battery. It's dug by hand at a Chinese-owned mining company in the Democratic Republic of Congo.

Preliminary processing is done on-site to produce cobalt hydroxide, which is then shipped to Dar es Salaam, Tanzania, and from there to China for the final stages of refining.

The cobalt is sold to companies that manufacture smartphone components in China, Japan, Taiwan, and Korea, as well as plants in Southeast Asia.

Japanese companies produce the majority of the mePhone's components: the special glass for the screen, the duplexer, SAW filter, power amplifier, and computer chip.

The top enclosure, bottom enclosure, and circuit board are manufactured in China, where the phone is also assembled.

From giant warehouses in Shenzhen, China, near Hong Kong, the phones are shipped to distribution centers in the mePhone's home country, the United States, and around the world.

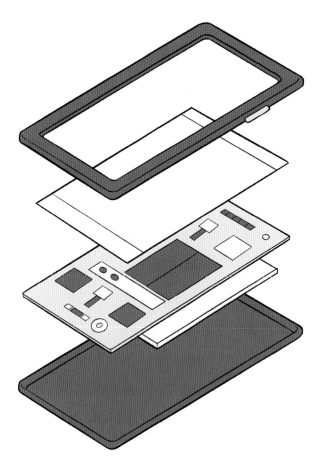

The distribution centers send the phones to retail stores, online sellers, and phone carriers.

As we can see, manufacturing electronics is now an international effort. The patents may be held by companies in North America, Europe, or Japan, but the products get made through a system like the one described above—known as a **supply chain**—which can circle the globe. The executives and owners of the companies that hold the patents reap most of the profits, with less going to companies and their workers as you move down the chain. Little is left for the workers who actually assemble the products.

MAKING MONEY FROM MONEY

For centuries, the economies of OECD countries were largely made up of industries that employed people to grow or make goods, such as wheat or cloth, or provide services, such as plumbing or health care.

Today, with the help of globalization and technology, well-to-do people can make money through a variety of new financial activities. This has increased the importance and power of finance within economies, a process known as **financialization**.

Studies show that the more "financialized" an economy, the more inequality there is in that country. Here are three examples that illustrate why this is.

> With incomes that have been stuck for decades, lower- and middle-class households have been relying more and more on loans to cover basic necessities and to buy assets—which are more likely to be the traditional kind, like a house.

NEW GAME, FEWER RULES

Starting in the 1980s, most OECD governments loosened the regulations, or rules, that control financial activities. In some countries, this **deregulation** helped create new types of assets that banks and other financial businesses can package and sell to investors for a fee. For example, to pay for a house, most families need a loan from a local bank, called a **mortgage**. The mortgage is repaid over many years, usually in monthly installments. After deregulation, banks began packaging thousands of mortgages together and selling the rights to those monthly payments to investors as a financial product.

Rich investors and financial businesses put enormous pressure on governments to keep deregulating the financial sector. But guess what happens when things go wrong? Who bails out the banks when investors have loaded up on "bad assets" that were not worth as much as they thought? That's right: governments.

A GROWING SECTOR

Deregulation led to the growth of the financial sector, which played a big part in increasing financialization. You're probably familiar with a few of the businesses and jobs in this sector: banks, insurance companies, accountants, tax lawyers. It also includes investment services—companies that make investments on behalf of clients. What unites all of these parts of the financial sector is that they make money from money.

Nice work if you can get it, but who gets it? The people who already have money! The financial sector is controlled by the richest citizens, who have the education and resources to make investments and take risks with those investments. They move money around the globe, investing in foreign companies. They try to predict future events, such as the price of oil—a prediction that can have an influence on its *actual* price and therefore how much oil is extracted from the ground. And they often chase quick profits, leaving the government to worry about the long-term health and stability of the economy.

PROFIT ABOVE ALL ELSE

In the seventeenth century, the Dutch East India Company became the first company to sell shares to the general public. Each share is a percentage of ownership in a company, with a price that goes up and down depending on how those who buy and sell those shares assess the company's value at any given moment. Share owners are known as shareholders, and they're entitled to a portion of the company's profits.

A company can make bigger profits by increasing revenue (selling more of their product or service) or decreasing costs (spending less on labor and parts).

Increased financialization has led to a mindset where the heads of companies (who own large amounts of shares) may prioritize shareholders' interests over the employees who work for them. Since lowering costs is one way to maximize profits, companies may spend less on workers. Another way companies boost the value of shares is buying some back when they have extra cash. By making fewer shares available for purchase to the public, share buybacks temporarily drive up the price of each share. This increases the wealth of shareholders, but critics say that it would be better for workers and the economy if companies used that extra cash for things like increasing wages or expanding the business to create more jobs.

In 2007, housing prices began to plummet, decreasing the value of assets tied to home mortgages and triggering a worldwide financial crisis. The European Central Bank (ECB) spent 2.6 trillion euros ($3 trillion USD) over almost four years buying up government and corporate debt—at a pace of 1.3 million euros per minute! That equates to roughly 7,600 euros for every person who uses the euro as currency.

THE TAKEAWAY

The evolution of work led to the development of the economic ladder. In particular, automation and globalization have contributed to growing inequality over the past four decades.

What Else We've Learned

 Our ancient ancestors may not have been as unequal as we are today.

 The introduction of agriculture may have been the root cause of widespread inequality.

 Automation and globalization increased inequality in some countries but also brought benefits, including less expensive products for consumers and raising many people in Asia out of poverty.

IDEAS IN ACTION

Many young people aren't waiting around for society to change for the better—they're making it happen. Opportunity Youth United is a national movement of young community leaders seeking to decrease poverty and increase opportunity across the United States. One of their signature programs is a network of "Community Action Teams"—youth led groups that tackle the most pressing issues in low-income areas of major American cities. The Sacramento, California, team hosted a town hall meeting with local officals to discuss youth and law enforcement and petitioned city council to invest more money in local youth programs.

LEARN MORE!

Opportunity Youth United
oyunited.org

Hadza Fund
hadzafund.org

"Animated History of Work," from MIT OpenCourseWare
youtube.com/watch?v=yBgKkYcoPgM

Follow Your Stuff: Who Makes It, Where Does It Come From, How Does It Get to You?, written by Kevin Sylvester and Michael Hlinka (Annick Press, 2019)

DIGGING DEEPER

When does unequal become unfair? Imagine two people are sharing a delicious cake and one takes a bigger slice. Unequal, sure, but is it unfair? Let's say the person with the bigger slice paid for the ingredients. Now let's say the person with the smaller slice did all the work of making the cake. What if the person with the bigger slice has a larger appetite? Or the person with a smaller slice hasn't eaten all day? Most people accept that there are inequalities in life, but our sense of fairness is shaped by our circumstances and our values, the things we think are important. How do you think an egalitarian society would—or should—slice up the cake? Equally, according to each person's needs or their contributions, or something else?

CHAPTER 5

More Than Money

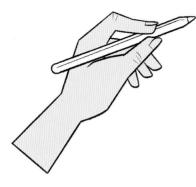

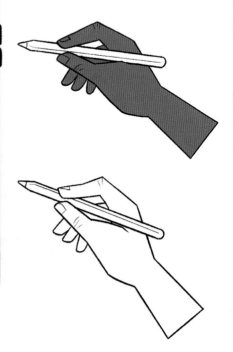

Introduction:

A DIFFERENT TYPE OF POVERTY

It started with a petition. That's how Amika George, who was seventeen at the time, launched a campaign called Free Periods. Its goal was to pressure the U.K. government to end "period poverty" and give free menstruation products to young people enrolled in programs that provide free school meals to low-income students. Over time, Free Periods has grown into a movement to ensure that anyone who menstruates, of any age, can get free or affordable menstruation products in the U.K.

What does this have to do with inequality? Financial poverty is the number one obstacle to buying these essential products. Without them, those who menstruate face a major barrier to going to school and work. Nearly 10 percent of students in the U.K. miss school regularly because they can't afford menstruation products. In poorer countries, they may lack access to toilets, water for washing, and information about their health.

Period poverty has a negative impact on a person's ability to get an education, earn income, and build wealth. Being forced out of school or work because you're having a period may hurt your self-confidence and sense of self-worth. It can create a sense of shame about periods and bodies. And it can reinforce the idea of girls and women as the "weaker sex" or that their place is in the home.

Period poverty has been around for centuries, and so it's only right that this chapter takes another quick trip back in time. We'll discover how economic inequality has been tied to inequality of power, influence, and opportunity for hundreds, even thousands, of years. In other words, we're going to explore why inequality has long been about a lot more than money.

THE SOCIAL LADDER

Like "inequality," the word "status" has more than one meaning.

It could refer to your relationship status with that special someone or the status of the job application you submitted to your favorite store at the mall. In economics, "status" may be used to describe your economic level—but it's never only about money.

Your economic and social level are closely linked. There's even a fancy term for it: **socioeconomic status**.

A person's socioeconomic status is determined by multiple factors: income, education level, job, and other things people value. Doctors and lawyers have a high status in most societies because they are well-educated, respected for their work, and earn good incomes. Sports stars have high status thanks to their elite skills and mega-salaries. Instagrammers and YouTubers can gain high status through high numbers of clicks and views. We treat royalty like celebrities and celebrities like royalty—that is, as if they somehow are above us all.

Your socioeconomic status can shape how you see and feel about yourself—your self-image and self-worth. This can have a profound effect on your mental health. It can also have a big impact on your future, for better and for worse.

Rich in Connections

Social capital is a special type of asset. You can't sell it like a house or stocks, but it does have an impact on your economic prospects. It refers to your wealth of social connections: the relationships and bonds you have with the people in your family, community, or culture. In less-equal countries, fewer people have social capital. Perhaps not coincidentally, studies have found they also have less trust among their citizens. In more-equal countries, where more people have social capital, we see more connections, cooperation, and trust. As well, in places that have less economic inequality and more social capital, you have a better chance of moving up in life.

The World Happiness Report, compiled annually by the United Nations, ranks countries by how happy their citizens perceive themselves to be. The majority of the most equal countries in the world are also ranked among the highest for happiness. This happiness appears to be fueled by strong social bonds and trust, generous government benefits, and optimism about the future.

Have you ever felt bad about yourself after peeking into someone else's life on social media? Comparing ourselves to others who may be better off can hurt self-esteem and cause anxiety.

When people feel their social status is threatened, their levels of the stress hormone cortisol shoot up. Higher cortisol increases your risk of health problems, including depression.

People who feel they have low economic status but a good chance of improving it feel less angry than those who are more pessimistic about their future.

When the next rung of the ladder seems out of reach, it may create what's known as "economic despair" and a sense of defeat. For example, low-income male students in the United States are more likely to drop out of high school in places where there is a greater gap between the low-income and middle-income levels.

More equal societies have lower rates of substance abuse and depression, both of which can affect a person's ability to improve their circumstances.

Some researchers believe that the link between inequality and violent crime is status. When income and wealth are low, a person's socioeconomic status—and therefore self-worth—may depend more on their social reputation. This can lead to aggression when that reputation is threatened, through insults and other perceived slights.

A CHANGE IN STATUS

As we learned in chapter 4, the arrival of large-scale agriculture began the division of people into "haves" and "have-nots."

Beyond how you earn your living, which group you fall into might be influenced by other parts of your social identity, such as your race, ethnicity, religion, or even where you were born. (We'll explore this in more detail in chapter 6.) A prime example is the oldest and most common identity label of them all: your **gender**.

DIFFERENT BUT EQUAL

All hunter-gatherer societies divide labor by gender—traditionally, male and female. Men do most or all of the hunting, while women do most or all of the gathering and child-rearing. But a society can still have equality among genders, even when they participate in different activities. Hadza women are free to choose their own husbands and to make decisions for themselves and their families.

PULLING THEIR WEIGHT

Anthropologists at the University of Cambridge examined the shape and strength of bones from women who lived in Central Europe during the Neolithic Age (5300–4600 BCE), Early and Middle Bronze Age (2300–1450 BCE), Iron Age (850 BCE–100 CE), and early Middle Ages (800-850 CE). The study, published in 2017, found that women in early agricultural societies had 5 to 10 percent more arm strength than modern female athletes, probably thanks to doing farm work alongside men.

THE PLOW THEORY

In the 1970s, Danish-French economist Ester Boserup proposed that the invention of the plow, about 4,000 years ago, pushed many women out of the fields. Controlling the machine and the large animals that pulled it required significant upper body strength, giving men an advantage, and it would have been impractical for women to plow fields with children underfoot. Her theory was that this new division of labor gave rise to the idea that a woman's place is in the home.

To test the plow theory, economists from the University of Southern Denmark and Aarhus University examined agricultural histories all over the world, comparing the number of years that a region's farmers had been using the plow by 1500 CE and its current level of gender equality. (They adjusted the data to take into account the fact that a plow wouldn't be a suitable farm tool in some geographical areas.) The 2015 study found that the societies that adopted the plow the earliest have fewer women in the workforce today and fewer women in government, and were later to give women the vote. They concluded that Boserup was onto something: the plow may have helped shape attitudes toward gender that have been harder to overcome the longer they've been around.

Organizations That Promote Gender Equality

Equality Now
equalitynow.org

GATE
gate.ngo

Global Fund for Women
globalfundforwomen.org

MenEngage Alliance
menengage.org

Plan International
plan-international.org

UN Women
unwomen.org/en

DIFFERENT BUT NOT EQUAL

Today, gender still plays a big part in shaping a person's social status and economic status.

Take the **pay gap**: in just about every country in the world, men get paid more than women for doing the same or similar work.

There are a number of potential reasons for this gap. Employers may undervalue female employees who can't work as many hours as men because they devote more time to raising their children. Women may lose opportunities to get ahead at work if they take maternity leave after having a baby. Even worse, employers may not offer opportunities to women in *anticipation* that they might eventually go on maternity leave or reduce their hours.

Women also fill caretaking occupations that don't have high salaries: childcare, eldercare, nursing, and social services. Unfortunately, because most workers are paid according to the profits they help produce, rather than the value of their work to society, women are often unpaid or underpaid for work that is essential to our families and communities.

 One reason some women earn less than their male coworkers is because they need to work fewer hours. To get a more accurate picture of the wage gap, it's better to compare the wages earned for every hour worked. For example, for every dollar earned by Canadian men, women earn an average of 87 cents.

South Korea has the highest gender pay gap in OECD countries (a 34.6 percent difference in earnings), and Costa Rica has one of the lowest (just 3 percent).

Differences in earnings don't just affect **cisgender** women. One study found that the earnings of **transgender** women drop by as much as a third after they transition from male to female. On the other hand, many transgender men earn as much or more after transitioning from female to male.

> "If wealth was the inevitable result of hard work and enterprise, every woman in Africa would be a millionaire."
> —George Monbiot, writer and activist

EFFECTIVE LEADERSHIP

Several of the countries with the most effective responses to the COVID-19 pandemic at its height had something unusual in common: female national leaders. Only about 10 percent of countries have women in the top job, but when researchers compared each of their pandemic outcomes to similar countries led by men, women-led countries came out ahead. These included New Zealand, Germany, Taiwan, and four of the five Nordic countries, all of which were able to slow the spread of the virus and minimize its economic consequences.

During the COVID-19 pandemic, women around the world reported taking on the bulk of homeschooling and other family duties during shutdowns, often while working from home. Women were twice as likely as men to be "essential workers" who continued to work outside the home when most workplaces were closed.

Did You Know?

Women do more than twice the unpaid labor of men, including cooking, cleaning, and taking care of their children and elderly relatives.

Before Covid-19, 55 percent of women were part of the workforce globally, compared with 82 percent of men.

In eighteen countries, men have the legal right to prevent their wives from working outside the home.

Dozens of countries have laws preventing women from performing certain jobs.

The United States is the only OECD country that doesn't offer paid maternity/paternity leave.

Every year a girl stays in school can add 14 percent to her future income.

Women are the majority of university students in more than one hundred countries . . .

. . . but 130 million girls around the world are not attending primary or secondary school.

THE TAKEAWAY

When it comes to inequality, your economic and social status go hand in hand, but it's important to remember that your socioeconomic status does not define who you are or your value as a person.

What Else We've Learned

 Your mental health and attitudes can have a big impact on upward mobility.

 Moving up social and economic ladders is extra challenging for some social groups.

In just about every country in the world, men are paid more than women for the same or similar work.

IDEAS IN ACTION

Justice for Girls is a Canadian charity that promotes equality, safety, and health for teenage girls who live in poverty, as well as freedom from violence and colonialism. It challenges laws and policies that violate young women's rights or liberties and promotes those that support them. It also makes recommendations to the criminal justice system to ensure that girls who are the victims of violence or are accused of crimes are treated safely and fairly as they move through each part of the system (the police, criminal courts, correctional facilities).

LEARN MORE!

Free Periods
freeperiods.org

Amika George
@AmikaGeorge

Justice for Girls
justiceforgirls.org

DIGGING DEEPER

Many nursing homes in Canada, the U.K., and the U.S. are staffed predominantly by immigrant women who tend to earn low wages. Are these women poorly paid just because they're women, immigrants, and/or people of color? There's no question that different aspects of a person's identity can lead to discrimination in the workplace, affecting who has power and who performs which jobs. But discrimination has been around for centuries, so it can't be the only explanation as to why economic inequality has worsened over the past forty years, for some people more than others and in some places more than others.

As we learned in chapter 4, three of the main drivers of increasing inequality are automation, globalization, and financialization. These "-ations" developed as businesses created operating models that increasingly prioritized profits for owners and investors, like nursing-home shareholders, over the people who work for them. This has had a greater impact on historically disadvantaged groups, who may have fewer employment opportunities and less power within the workplace. In the end, you can't completely separate discrimination from the other "-ations": they are all part of the larger picture.

In 2020, three companies that run nursing homes in the Canadian province of Ontario received a total of $138 million CAD ($109 million USD) from the provincial government to help pay frontline workers who had to continue working during the pandemic. Later that year, the companies paid out $171 million CAD ($135 million USD) to shareholders.

CHAPTER 6

BORN INTO IT

Introduction:

PLAYING THE ODDS

In more-equal societies, most people have chances to move up in life, regardless of their socioeconomic status at birth. In less-equal societies, people may be born into advantages that give them a boost or face disadvantages that can make it hard to get past the starting line. The less equal the country, the more those advantages and disadvantages matter.

Remember Isaiah from chapter 3? He was exceptional because he moved from the lower-income level into the middle level, and continues to climb toward the upper level. But that's only half the story. As a Black American, Isaiah faced more obstacles to upward mobility than most—just one of the disadvantages experienced by Black Americans that were highlighted by the protests that began sweeping the United States in the spring of 2020.

The COVID-19 pandemic was still in full swing when large crowds took to the streets in all fifty states and more than a dozen cities around the world to protest the killing of an unarmed Black man named George Floyd by police in Minneapolis, Minnesota. The protests were held under the banner of the Black Lives Matter movement, which calls out police brutality and the unfair treatment of Black Americans in the criminal justice system. For example, predominantly Black neighborhoods are more heavily policed. Black Americans are more likely to be arrested, and more likely to be incarcerated, and serve longer sentences than white Americans for the same or similar offenses. Black men in particular are far more likely to be killed by police.

But the inequality doesn't stop there. Due to discriminatory laws, policies, and hiring practices that go back hundreds of years, Black Americans have a lower average income than white Americans, as well as significantly less wealth. How much less? The average white household has eight times the wealth of the average Black family. These disadvantages—and many others—have a major impact on quality of life and prospects for a better future.

This chapter introduces key advantages and disadvantages that we may have from birth, from details about your parents to where you live. It also looks at extra barriers that minority groups and marginalized communities must overcome, and tackles the myth that all you need to be as successful as Isaiah is to work hard and dream big.

WIRED FOR SUCCESS?

One of the biggest advantages in life is being born into a family that's financially secure.

The better off your parents are, the better your odds of staying high on, or climbing, the economic ladder. But why? Is it because the game is rigged in favor of richer people? Or because you inherited traits from your parents that might make you more likely to succeed?

There's little question that genetics—the biological characteristics you inherit from your parents—contribute to your talents, personality, and ability to develop skills that may help you along in life. However, it can be difficult to separate the influence of someone's genetics from the influence of the environment they grew up in. A child who was born with a learning disability, for instance, has a better chance of achieving a high level of education if her family can afford to give her the extra help she needs.

A group of economists from Sweden, Ireland, and the United States investigated how much genetics can predict your future wealth. They reviewed economic data for adopted children in Sweden, comparing the wealth of their biological parents to that of their adoptive parents. They then looked at each child's net worth when they reached middle age. They discovered that children adopted by wealthy parents were more likely to become wealthy themselves. This was true even of children who had not yet inherited any wealth from their parents. Even though Sweden is one of the most equal countries in the world, the level of wealth in the homes the children were raised in was the biggest predictor of their financial future.

> "It is cruel jest to say to a bootless man that he ought to lift himself by his own bootstraps."
> —Martin Luther King, Jr.

> "In the 1800s, the expression 'pull oneself up by the bootstraps' meant the opposite of what it does now," writes *New York Times* journalist Nicholas Kristof. "Then it was used mockingly to describe an impossible act."

MYTH OF THE SELF-MADE PERSON

The United States has the most billionaires of any country, nearly 700 of them. Among these billionaires are people who overcame incredible odds to become so successful. Look at Oprah Winfrey, born into poverty in rural Mississippi and now one of the wealthiest people in America. Or Kylie Jenner, once thought to be the youngest "self-made billionaire," who rose from humble beginnings as a highly paid reality-TV star to start her own cosmetics company and . . . never mind. When it comes to upward mobility, "self-made" means only that a person didn't inherit most of their wealth, not that they pulled themselves up the economic ladder all on their own. And plenty of billionaires did inherit their wealth. Nearly a third in the United States, and more than half in Europe, got their fortunes from the Bank of Mom and Dad.

> The word "fortune" is derived from the Latin word *Fortuna*, goddess of luck or chance.

Me? Privileged?

When you've grown up in a low-income family, it can be hard to understand how anyone could claim you have privilege, which is another way of saying "advantage." For example, how can there be "white privilege" when so many white families live below the poverty line? Think of it this way: some people are from low-income households *and* have to deal with discrimination and other problems that make inequality even worse. It's the absence of these additional challenges that is the privilege.

HOME TEAM ADVANTAGE

If you want to be born lucky, choose your parents wisely.

Richer families can give their kids benefits that set them up for success, such as living in a "good" neighborhood and professional connections that can help them with their future careers. They are also better able to provide educational opportunities, which help kids to help themselves.

THE SPENDING GAP
Researchers from the University of California, Berkeley, and Colorado State University found that as income inequality has grown in the United States, richer families have increased their spending on things like childcare, lessons, and extracurricular activities for their children compared to poorer families.

THE SUMMER SLIDE
Poorer students have fewer books at home, are less likely to be enrolled in summer activities that boost education, and are less likely to have opportunities to read with their parents or on their own over the summer break. Not reading during the summer holiday can cause reading skills to backslide, putting poorer students at a disadvantage in the new school year.

OCCUPATIONAL ADVANTAGE
A 2018 UNICEF report on education in OECD countries found that children who have at least one parent working in a "professional occupation" (e.g., engineer, nurse, or manager) have significantly higher reading scores than those who don't.

EQUALITY OF EDUCATION
In less-equal countries, children whose parents have high levels of education earn 20 percent more as adults than those whose parents have less education. In more-equal countries, a child's own education has more impact on her future income than her parents'. As well, more-equal countries often make a university education free or relatively affordable, which means students are less likely to be saddled with student debt after they graduate.

SECOND CHANCES

It takes time to adjust to a new country, especially for immigrants coping with a new language, culture, or education system, as well as financial challenges. In OECD countries with high levels of immigration, young immigrants tend to fare less well in school at age fifteen than students who are not immigrants. In several nations, this is true of second-generation immigrants—those born after their parents moved to a new country. However, in Canada, some second-generation immigrant groups perform *better* academically than non-immigrants and they have equally good odds of upward mobility. This suggests that both the country their parents came from and where they immigrated to makes a difference.

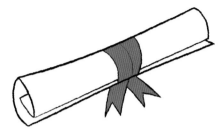

ONE OR TWO

Statistics show that children who grow up with two parents in the same household have a better chance of upward mobility than children raised in single-parent households. They may also be more likely to achieve a higher level of education. This doesn't mean that single parents aren't good parents. At least part of this difference is because a single parent may have less money and time to invest in their children compared to a two-parent household, and not enough support from the government and their community.

When Teens Become Parents

Girls from poorer families are more likely to become teenage mothers than girls from higher-income families, and many of these young mothers will remain trapped in poverty throughout their lives. Becoming a parent at a young age has been cited as the main reason why it's so difficult for teens to improve their financial circumstances. However, a study from the National Bureau of Economic Research in the U.S. found that teen mothers in America tend not to be worse off later in life than girls who were born into poverty and did not have children as teens. This means that being born poor, not becoming a parent, is why young moms may stay poor.

LOCATION, LOCATION, LOCATION

As we saw on the Great Gatsby Curve (on pages 34–35), you have a better chance at upward mobility when you grow up in a more equal country.

But it's not just about the passport you hold— where you live *within* your country matters, too.

Vancouver, Canada, has a higher percentage of residents who live below the poverty line compared to most Canadian cities, but it has one of the highest mobility rates in the country. There may be more children born into poverty in Vancouver, but they have a relatively good chance of moving up the economic ladder.

Nearby Squamish has far less poverty than Vancouver, but it has one of the lowest mobility rates in the country. That's in part because the town lost its biggest employers when the sawmill, logging operation, and pulp mill shut down. There simply aren't a lot of opportunities for younger workers to move into higher-paying jobs than those held by their parents without leaving the community.

REGIONAL DIFFERENCES

In every country, some regions are richer and some are poorer. Much of this is due to the industries that employ people in those regions. In recent decades, places that rely on agriculture and manufacturing for jobs have fared less well than those that have more jobs (and often better-paying jobs) in technology and finance. Consequently, these richer regions may also have better health care, education, and government programs to support people in need.

Redlining is the practice of denying people in a particular area the opportunity to become homeowners, by refusing to provide them with loans, mortgages, or insurance. Though redlining has been outlawed in the United States for decades, it helped create the wealth gaps between Black and white populations, as well as neighborhoods divided by race, which persist today.

In Singapore, 80 percent of residents live in housing built and supported by government. To prevent the return of cultural tensions from the past, the government requires each apartment building to have a mix of tenants from the main ethnic groups in the city, including Chinese, Malay, and Indian. This keeps neighborhoods from becoming divided along ethnic lines.

YOUR 'HOOD

Most cities are organized, to a degree, into more prosperous and disadvantaged neighborhoods. The more prosperous neighborhoods may be cleaner and have higher-quality housing, more public spaces, lower crime rates, and more opportunities to take part in community and cultural events. Problem is, when these neighborhoods are created by richer people sticking together, they leave poorer people out in the cold. Living in a disadvantaged neighborhood not only deprives you of these benefits, but it can affect your sense of well-being and optimism, which in turn can affect your future.

WHY NOT MOVE?

Research into an American project called "Moving to Opportunity" found that children of low-income families who moved to more prosperous neighborhoods before the age of thirteen earned higher incomes in adulthood. So, if moving can help, why don't more people do it? For starters, moving costs money that low-income families may not have to spare. The farther you move, the more likely it is that the family income earners are going to have to find new jobs. Mortgages and rents are higher in more prosperous neighborhoods, and they're becoming less and less affordable in the biggest cities around the world. Just as importantly, people want to stay where they have roots—family, friends, and community. Moving might bring opportunities, but it might be too high a price in other respects.

LIVING IN THE MARGINS

As we learned in chapter 5, some social groups may have additional hurdles to upward mobility.

In addition to discrimination faced at school, work, or in the community, your social identity may make you more or less likely to experience disadvantages that affect your odds of moving up the economic ladder. Here are just a few examples of the challenges faced by those living in the margins of society:

IMMIGRANTS AND REFUGEES

When immigrants and refugees arrive in their new country, they find their education and professional credentials are not recognized which means they have to settle for lower-paying jobs.

People who come from places that are wracked by war, violence, and corruption may struggle to adapt to their new circumstances.

Low incomes, language barriers, discrimination, and lack of support within their adopted community can make adapting even more difficult.

RACIAL/ETHNIC IDENTITY

Minority racial and ethnic groups may experience discrimination throughout their education and work lives. For example, Black American boys are more likely than white boys to be removed from the classroom for bad behavior, just as Black men are more likely to be incarcerated than white men for the same crimes. Some research shows that when Black Americans remove references to their race on resumes, they may be twice as likely to secure a job interview. Once in a job, they often receive lower salaries than their white counterparts and are less likely to be promoted. Minority racial and ethnic groups are also more likely to experience disadvantages that are difficult for anyone to overcome, be that growing up in a single-parent household or less affluent families and neighborhoods.

The historical disadvantages experienced by Black communities have been exacerbated by the economic developments of the past few decades, especially the loss of good-paying jobs that, in previous eras, could have lifted families into the middle class and beyond.

SEXUAL/GENDER IDENTITY

LGBTQ2+ youth are at higher risk of becoming homeless when they are young.

A survey of trans and non-binary people conducted by Trans PULSE Canada found that half of respondents between the ages of about twenty-five and fifty earned $30,000 CAD ($24,000 USD) or less per year, compared to an average of $58,000 CAD ($46,000 USD) for the general population of Canada within the same age range.

In many countries, LGBTQ2+ people cannot marry, which excludes them from certain economic advantages, such as sharing insurance and **tax credits**.

DISABILITY

People with disabilities are more likely to fall below the poverty line. In Canada, people with disabilities are 50 percent more likely to live in poverty than those without disabilities.

The need for assistive technology and extra tutoring can create practical barriers to performing well at school and work.

The amounts governments spend supporting people with disabilities vary hugely across OECD countries. Denmark, Sweden, and Norway invest more than twice as much per capita as Japan, the United States, the United Kingdom, and Canada.

Realigning the Starting Blocks

While Black Americans have, on average, lower incomes and less wealth than white Americans, something interesting happens when you compare Black girls and white girls who grew up at the same income level. When their starting blocks are aligned, they tend to end up with similar incomes in adulthood.

Unfortunately, it appears that the disadvantages experienced by Black boys and men may be harder to overcome. When you compare the outcomes for Black boys and white boys who grew up in similar circumstances, white boys tend to pull ahead later in life. The reasons for this and the best way to address it need more study, but research indicates that Black boys have a better chance of upward mobility in neighborhoods with a higher-than-average presence of Black fathers and—unsurprisingly—less racial prejudice.

AN UNHEALTHY DIVIDE

The disadvantages suffered by people from marginalized communities are vividly illustrated in an area of utmost importance to all of us: our health.

Just a few weeks into the COVID-19 pandemic, scientists began to notice a disturbing trend: some patients seemed to be at greater risk for severe illness and death. These included the elderly and those already coping with serious health issues.

One of the first states in America to release COVID-19 data by race was Louisiana. It reported that Black citizens make up 33 percent of its population but 70 percent of those who had died from the virus to date. Similarly alarming statistics began to crop up across the country. In addition to Black victims, Latinx people and low-income people of all races were disproportionately represented among the dead. At one point, members of the Navajo Nation had the highest **per capita** infection rate in the country.

COVID-19 shone a spotlight on the ways that inequality in health and health care mirror other forms of inequality. People who live in poverty are more likely to suffer from health conditions that make a virus like COVID-19 more deadly. And patients at all economic levels may face discrimination from health-care providers based on their gender, race, ethnicity, sexual orientation, ability, economic level, or existing health problems.

The National Institutes of Health in the United States created a video titled "Social Inequalities in Health," which explains the different types, causes, and consequences of inequality in health care: nih.gov/file/3921.

DISCRIMINATION IN HEALTH CARE

Research studies and medical training are performed more often with male subjects than female subjects and with white patients than people of color.

Homeless people and those with mental illness and addictions can be misdiagnosed because symptoms are assumed to be something else, such as intoxication.

Studies in New Zealand, Australia, and Canada revealed that Indigenous peoples don't always receive timely care because of poor communication between health-care providers and patients, and a tendency for health-care providers to blame patients for causing their own health problems.

One study found that more than 56 percent of lesbian, gay, and bisexual patients and 70 percent of transgender patients have received inadequate health care because a medical provider refused to treat them due to personal or religious beliefs.

Black women in America are three to four times more likely to die from having a baby than white women, and Black infants are twice as likely as white infants to die before their first birthday. Some researchers believe that health-care providers don't always take Black women as seriously as white women when they report symptoms.

Activities promoting health and preventative care frequently overlook people with disabilities. For example, young people with disabilities may be excluded from sex-education programs.

During the COVID-19 pandemic, keeping your distance from other people—known as "social distancing"—was key to stopping the spread of the virus. That wasn't so difficult if you lived in a house, especially one with a yard where you could get fresh air and hang out with friends and family outdoors. Social distancing was a lot harder for those living in, say, an apartment building. In OECD countries, nearly one in three lower-income kids live in crowded places where it can be hard to maintain social distance in hallways, elevators, stairwells, and small, shared outdoor spaces.

THE TAKEAWAY

As noted in chapter 5, statistics do not determine your fate. Being born into advantages doesn't mean you shouldn't get credit for putting in the necessary work to achieve your goals, and facing disadvantages doesn't mean your dreams are out of reach. But if we don't acknowledge these advantages and disadvantages, we may never realign the starting blocks for those who weren't born lucky.

What Else We've Learned

 While your genetic traits have an impact on your natural talents, the financial well-being of your parents can be a better predictor of your future income and wealth.

 The less equal the country, the more the advantages or disadvantages you may have from birth impact your quality of life and chances of upward mobility.

✓ In addition to many forms of discrimination, marginalized communities are more likely to experience disadvantages that would impact anyone's odds of upward mobility.

IDEAS IN ACTION

Brooklyn Owen of Jacksonville, Florida, went viral when one of her high school teachers started a GoFundMe campaign to pay for her college tuition. Before her gender transition, when she identified as gay and male, the high school valedictorian's family refused to accept her sexual orientation, finally forcing her out of their home over religious differences. When she raised seven times more funds than needed, she started the Unbroken Horizons Scholarship Foundation for LGBTQ2+ students from marginalized communities.

THE PLAYLIST

"Born This Way"–Lady Gaga

"Electric Avenue"–Eddy Grant

"I Can't Breathe"–H.E.R.

"The Virus"–The Halluci Nation

"Watch These Hands"–Sean Forbes

"The Way It Is"–Bruce Hornsby

LEARN MORE!

Unbroken Horizons Foundation
@unbrokenhorizons

OECD: Social and Welfare Issues
oecd.org/social

United Nations, Department of Economic and Social Affairs: Social Inclusion
un.org/development/desa/dspd

The World Bank: Social Sustainability and Inclusion
worldbank.org/en/topic/socialsustainability

CHAPTER 7

The Role of Government

Introduction:

A CAUSE . . . AND A SOLUTION

Autumn Peltier had to stand on a stool to reach the microphone the first time she spoke at the United Nations headquarters in New York City in March of 2018. Just thirteen years old and five feet tall, she may have needed a lift to be heard, but her message reached governments around the world. "No one should have to worry if the water is clean or if they will run out of water," she told the UN General Assembly, which is

By age fourteen, Autumn Peltier was appointed Chief Water Commissioner by the Anishinabek Nation, a political coalition of forty First Nations.

comprised of dignitaries from its 193 member states. "We all have a right to this water as we need it. Not just rich people, all people."

Autumn had been invited to speak at the launch of the UN's International Decade for Action on Water for Sustainable Development, an issue that's been close to her heart since she was a middle-schooler. A member of Wiikwemkoong First Nation in Ontario, Canada, she was alerted to the problem of contaminated water while attending a water ceremony at another First Nation reserve. She spotted signs in a washroom warning that the water was not safe to drink, just as it is in dozens of First Nations communities across the country. Autumn became determined to raise awareness of the crisis.

Indigenous peoples own or control land collectively—in groups—caring for approximately 22 percent of the world's land surface. They protect up to 80 percent of global **biodiversity**, including fragile ecosystems, and have been among the first to experience the destructive effects of climate change. It's no wonder Indigenous youth like Autumn Peltier are at the forefront of environmental and climate change activism.

By the time Autumn addressed the UN, she had become a prominent voice for water safety and rights. In 2015, she'd traveled all the way to Sweden to speak at the Children's Climate Conference. But environmental problems—and the inequalities they contribute to—can't be solved by activists alone. She needed to take her message to the people we elect to create policies, programs, laws, and regulations that protect our planet: governments. In fact, the actions governments take—or their lack of

Along with Black Americans, Indigenous peoples in America have the lowest rates of upward mobility in the United States. The mobility rates are also poor for Indigenous peoples in Canada, Australia, and New Zealand.

action—are often what cause environmental crises to begin with. And they are also key to solving them. The same could be said of just about every issue related to inequality, from education and health care to housing and workers' rights.

Over the next three chapters, we're going to look at ways to take on inequality, starting with government actions as both a cause and a solution. This chapter will be a crash course in how governments work and the challenges they face. We'll examine how politics influence a government's priorities and how they pay for programs that address inequality. Finally, we'll learn about how governments use laws and regulations to protect workers and ensure young people and their families can make ends meet.

Around the globe, lower-income people are more likely to live in hazardous conditions and to be the most affected by climate change. They have less influence in creating laws and government policies that address environmental issues and inequality. This is certainly true of Indigenous peoples, who make up about 5 percent of the world's population but about 15 percent of those living in extreme poverty.

WHAT'S POLITICS GOT TO DO WITH IT?

You might think it should be easy for governments to decide how to support those in need. Clean drinking water, affordable education, free meals so children don't go hungry—seems pretty basic, right?

But getting things done in government requires cooperation between people who may have different ideas and priorities. That's where politics comes into it.

Lobbying is the attempt to persuade the government to introduce, change, or get rid of laws and policies in order to benefit the lobbyist's interests.

COMPETING BELIEFS

Politicians, elected by voters, decide government actions. Most politicians belong to a political party, which is made up of individuals and groups who share interests and beliefs about the job of government. These common concerns help determine which issues will be treated as the most important. They also guide decisions about which programs to invest in and how to pay for them.

UNDER PRESSURE

Unfortunately, politicians face pressure from outside forces. This may come from corporations, especially those that employ a lot of people, or industries that are important to a politician's region. Oil and gas companies have spent millions of dollars lobbying against climate change policies that could lower their profits. These kinds of pressures have had a major impact on government actions.

Indigenous communities are on the frontlines of a battle between economics and the environment. Corporations lobby governments for access to land, water, and other natural resources, with promises of economy-boosting jobs. Environmental activists push back against projects that hand resources over to private companies or can cause harm to ecosystems. Indigenous peoples are often caught in the middle, thanks to treaty rights that may grant them control over resources and a share of the money earned from them.

COMMON GROUND

In many northern European countries, no single political party controls the government. Voters elect local politicians to represent them as members of **parliament**. Normally in a parliamentary system, the political party that has the most elected members takes control. Some countries, though, follow a system of "proportional representation," where even small parties can be granted a share of power based on the number of votes they receive. In these cases, coalitions may form, with parties agreeing to govern together. This requires compromise and teamwork and makes it more likely that a broader range of interests will be represented within the government.

The number of Americans who lost their health insurance when they lost their jobs during the COVID-19 pandemic was roughly the same as the number who gained insurance through the Affordable Care Act. In effect, the pandemic did what the Republican Party could not: rolled back the Affordable Care Act.

Public or Private?

In the United States, health care is mostly paid for through private health insurance companies. For a little over half the population, the cost is covered by employers. If your job doesn't come with this benefit, you have to pay for private insurance or join a public insurance program.

In 2010, the Democratic Party passed the Affordable Care Act. Among other things, the act made private insurance more affordable for those with lower incomes, and expanded Medicaid, a public insurance program for people with low incomes and disabilities. It also lowered the cost of prescription drugs for seniors enrolled in Medicare, which provides medical care for people over the age of sixty-five.

Some Democrats believe the federal government should pay for all or most health care through public insurance. This would help ensure everyone receives an equal level of care. (The U.S. is the only rich country that doesn't have a universal health-care system.) However, the Republican Party believes that patients should continue to obtain insurance through private companies. Some Republicans have proposed that the federal government play an even smaller role in health care by sending a set amount of money to individual states and letting state governments decide how to use it.

Although the Affordable Care Act helped millions of Americans get health-care insurance, the inability of the two parties to come to an agreement means millions more still have no health coverage at all.

THE DREADED T-WORD

Being in charge is tougher than it looks.
You've got to deal with the competing priorities of political parties.

Industries and activists lobby for government actions, which can conflict with one another. Then there are the regular folks who elected you, reporting that their water isn't clean or childcare is too expensive. You might decide that addressing inequality is your top priority, but how are you supposed to pay for equality-boosting programs? One answer is among the most hated words in the English language: taxes.

WHO PAYS?

Decisions about what to tax and at what rate are determined by the balance of political forces in a country or region. Some of the biggest political battles have been over personal income taxes, which are the largest source of money received by governments in most OECD countries. Here are three personal income tax models that show the vastly different approaches that governments can take.

Bottom heavy: Low taxes on the top income-distribution levels

The less the rich are taxed, the theory goes, the more money they can invest. These investments may boost the economy, and a healthy economy is good for everyone. Critics say that increasing inequality in countries where the rich don't pay their fair share is proof that only the top earners benefit from this approach. They point out that wealthy people are increasingly making investments that don't benefit the average household or the economy, as discussed in chapter 4 (pages 52-53), and that less tax from the rich means less money for governments to spend on public goods.

Top heavy: High taxes on the top income-distribution levels

By taking a larger share from the people who can most afford it, taxes can be used to help those at the middle- and bottom-income levels. This is known as redistribution. Those who oppose this system say that richer people shouldn't have to pay for government programs they don't need, that it punishes top earners for their success and therefore discourages people from "hard work" and risk-taking.

Tiered: Taxation rates go up with your income

This is known as a marginal tax system. For example, you might pay 15 percent on the first $50,000 of taxable income you earn, 20 percent on the next $50,000, 27 percent on the next $50,000, and so on. The middle class pays a lot into this type of system, but tends to benefit from the programs their taxes support. Political figures who support marginal tax systems have suggested swapping a steep increase in rates for a wealth tax on the richest citizens (a percentage of their net worth).

Ultimately, there is no absolute right or wrong when it comes to taxes, but there are competing ideas about what the government should pay for and which system is the best way to do it.

Over the past forty years, many OECD countries have lowered the tax rates on personal and business income. During the same period, they've doubled the amount of revenue they receive from taxes charged on goods and services. This has had a bigger impact on poorer people, who spend—rather than invest—most of their income.

THE DOUBLE IRISH DUTCH SANDWICH

No matter which taxation system a government uses, richer people have tools and tricks to avoid taxes that poorer people don't. Loopholes and deductions within tax laws can disproportionately help the wealthy. Individuals and businesses may also stash their assets in **tax havens**: countries that charge little or no taxes and share little to no information with other governments.

Alphabet Inc. is the U.S.-based parent company of Google and has subsidiaries (or "daughter companies") around the world. In a 2015 tax-avoidance scheme known as the "Double Irish Dutch Sandwich," it moved a portion of its revenues to Google Ireland Ltd.

. . . which sent the money to Google Netherlands Holdings B.V.

. . . which transferred it to Google Ireland Holdings Unlimited

. . . which was **incorporated** in Ireland but is officially a resident of

. . . Bermuda, where the company is managed and controlled and should pay its taxes. Coincidentally, no doubt, Bermuda has a zero percent corporate tax rate.

Confused? That's exactly the point. If no one knows how much money a company or individual makes because they're hiding it, how can they be taxed fairly?

Some tax-avoidance schemes, including the "Double Irish Dutch Sandwich," have been phased out, but not all. Governments could demand more transparency from corporations like Google. They could create an international registry of assets that keeps track of who owns what. They could insist that companies pay taxes in each country where they make money. But change has been slow because powerful people put pressure on politicians to keep things as is. To further complicate matters, some countries have cut the budgets of their tax agencies in recent years, making it harder to investigate tax avoidance on an international scale. This deprives governments of money that could pay for public programs that address inequality.

Taxes can be used to shape people's behaviors. High taxes on cigarettes discourage smoking and prevent diseases that place a burden on the health-care system. Similarly, it's thought that carbon taxes on gasoline may help reduce pollution by making it more expensive to drive.

GETTING BY

Of course, governments do more than just tax and spend.
Another important function is writing laws and regulations
that help society run smoothly and keep people safe.

They create rules that protect the environment from pollution, and marginalized communities from discrimination. They set safety standards for workplaces and place restrictions on the use of young workers. They decide the maximum number of hours people should work and the minimum amount they should be paid.

Between 1939 and 1972, the government in Queensland, Australia, seized the wages of more than 10,000 low-paid Indigenous workers, including farmhands, domestic workers, and kitchen staff. Acting as the workers' "protector," the government supposedly put the earnings into **trust accounts,** but some of the wages were never released to workers. In 2019, the state government settled a **class action suit** by agreeing to pay $190 million AUD to the workers and their descendants.

JUST ENOUGH

Laws that set the lowest wage an employer can pay a worker were first introduced in Australia and New Zealand in the 1890s. Their main purpose was to stop the exploitation of laborers in factories, especially women and children working long hours for little pay. Today, many OECD countries have minimum-wage laws. The rate may be set by federal and/or regional governments and reflect the cost of living in each area.

Political parties, economists, and researchers often disagree about whether minimum wage helps or hurts the economy. A common argument is that a higher minimum wage makes it more likely that employers will reduce an employee's hours, replace labor with technology, or eliminate jobs altogether. A counterargument is that recent research shows increases to the minimum wage have not reduced the number of jobs predicted and that higher wages mean workers have more money to spend—which boosts the economy.

BELOW THE MINIMUM

Researchers at the University of British Columbia in Vancouver found that teen employees who worked part-time while finishing their education were more likely than those without jobs to earn a higher salary later in life. The 2014 study also found that young workers were more likely to end up in a profession that was a good match for their interests and talents. The researchers attributed this to young adults learning important skills and discovering their own particular strengths while on the job.

How much they should be paid for that job, however, is another political debate, with some governments setting minimum wages for teenagers that are lower than those for adults.

Stuck in the Past

In the United States, employers have to pay their employees a minimum hourly wage that is set by the federal, state, or local government, depending on the industry. The federal wage didn't change for more than a decade—but the cost of living went up by 19 percent, making life more difficult for 30 million low-wage workers.

EMPLOYEE of the MONTH

2009: $7.25 per hour

EMPLOYEE of the MONTH

2019: $7.25 per hour

THE TAKEAWAY

All governments face disagreements about the best way to run the country, but the governments of more-equal countries have one thing in common: they have agreed to invest in programs that support the middle class and assist those at the bottom of the economic ladder.

What Else We've Learned

 Politicians and political parties receive a lot of outside pressure from lobbyists trying to influence government policies.

 If there is political will, taxes can pay for government programs that address inequality—but not everyone pays their fair share.

 Governments protect workers through laws and regulations, but not all workers receive equal protection.

IDEAS IN ACTION

Amelia Telford was in high school when she became involved with the Australian Youth Climate Coalition, an alliance of twenty-five youth-led organizations taking on the climate crisis. After graduation, she founded Seed, the country's first Indigenous youth climate network, to give young Indigenous activists a louder voice in the climate change movement. Seed spearheads a number of campaigns that aim to protect the environment from the destructive effects of oil and gas exploration, and stands up for the rights of Indigenous peoples as care-takers of the land.

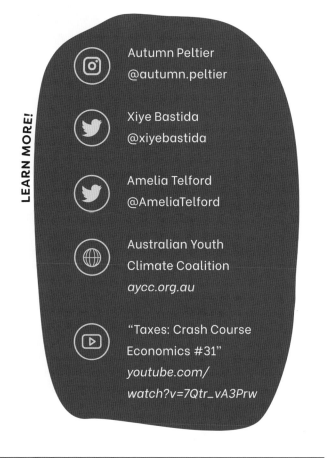

LEARN MORE!

Autumn Peltier
@autumn.peltier

Xiye Bastida
@xiyebastida

Amelia Telford
@AmeliaTelford

Australian Youth
Climate Coalition
aycc.org.au

"Taxes: Crash Course
Economics #31"
*youtube.com/
watch?v=7Qtr_vA3Prw*

CONSIDER THIS

"One time a politician asked me to have a recorded conversation with them. Turns out they just wanted me to ask *them* questions . . . The problem with this type of one-sided conversations is that we don't get to ask questions, we don't get to express what we want from the government, and our view of you doesn't change bc we have already studied your policy—we just need you to make it better." —Twitter posts by Xiye Bastida, Climate Justice Activist

CHAPTER 8

Closing the Gap

Introduction:

INEQUALITY IS NOT INEVITABLE

THE TRINH FAMILY

Great-grandfather: Construction laborer

Great-grandmother: Cleaner

Grandfather: Assembly-line worker at a car factory

Grandmother: Homemaker

Father: Assembly-line worker at a car factory

After factory closed, retrained as a mechanic

Mother: Daycare worker

Lãng: High school senior

Ben: High school senior

When the Trinh family settled in Canada, they began a classic tale of upward mobility, with each generation moving further up the economic ladder than the one before it. One of its youngest members, Ben, always thought he'd follow his father and grandfather into a well-paying job at the local car assembly plant. But the plant closed, its jobs sent south to Mexico.

Ben's grades are good enough to get into university or community college, but unlike his twin sister, Lãng, he's not likely to go on full scholarship. Now Ben worries that he might be the first person in his family facing *downward* mobility.

Will he?

Ben lives in Canada, which is in the middle of the pack when you compare inequality among OECD countries. The odds of upward mobility in Canada are twice that of the United States and United Kingdom, which some economists credit to Canada's high-quality public school systems. That gives Ben a leg up even before he graduates high school.

Universities and colleges in Canada are much less expensive than in the U.S. and the U.K. (though more expensive than the free or low-cost schools of countries like Norway). This could make it more affordable for Ben to get the post-secondary education and skills training he'll need to secure a good job without taking on an unmanageable amount of student debt.

Canada has relatively strong youth labor laws and government-funded resources for young workers, which could help Ben if he decides to work part-time while continuing his studies.

So, while Ben may face hurdles that his parents didn't, he still has every reason to feel optimistic about the future.

Ben's example is another reminder of something we've been talking about since the Great Gatsby Curve appeared in chapter 3: where you live has an impact on your ability to overcome inequality. It also demonstrates what the Hadza taught us in chapter 4: inequality might be everywhere but it's not inevitable.

We're going to take a closer look at four issues related to inequality and the public goods that can help people overcome it, including education, workers' rights, health, and housing. As we've learned, disadvantages in these areas can create barriers to upward mobility, but the equality-promoting actions highlighted in this chapter show us that—with enough political will and creative thinking—governments, organizations, activists, and individuals have the power to do something about it.

LEARNING FROM THE BEST

As Ben Trinh reminded us in the introduction, a good-quality public education can improve your chances of upward mobility.

Public education is funded by governments, a way of ensuring that all young people in a country or region have the opportunity to go to school. But just because everyone can get a public education doesn't mean they'll get an equally good one.

In the United States, many school districts are divided along racial lines. About half the country's students live in districts where more than 75 percent of students are either white or people of color. The districts where Black Americans make up the majority of the population often have less funding for education and, consequently, a lower standard of education.

Let's compare the education systems in two countries—Japan and the United States—to see why Japan ranks with Canada among the top education systems for grades K–12 in the world, while the United States keeps falling further behind.

GETTING SCHOOLED

In Japan, only about 10 percent of differences in academic performances may be caused by differences in students' socioeconomic statuses. In the United States, it's 17 percent. That's largely because Japan offers the same school system throughout the country, so that all students, no matter where they live, have an equal shot at a good education. The U.S.? Not so much.

JAPAN

- Teachers are hired and paid by the national and prefectural governments (similar to state or provincial governments).

- Early in their careers, teachers move every three years to ensure they are matched to the schools that need them most. Strong teachers are matched with disadvantaged students.

- Teachers' salaries, along with building expenses and other costs, are fairly consistent across the country, based on the cost of living in the area where the school is located.

- The teaching profession requires a high level of training and qualifications, and teachers are paid more than the OECD average.

- Japan spends less on education than the U.S. but has better academic outcomes.

- Costs are kept down through a variety of savings measures. For example, most schools are built according to the same simple design model.

Indspire is a Canadian charity led by Indigenous people for Indigenous people. It raises funds to support post-secondary education for First Nations, Inuit, and Métis students, and provides additional support through research, peer support groups, and mentoring programs. After the federal government, it is the largest funder of Indigenous education in the country.

At age nine, Asean Johnson of Chicago successfully fought to keep his school open after the city announced plans to shutter fifty-four public schools. He persuaded those in power with passionate speeches, including one at the fiftieth anniversary of the March on Washington (at which Martin Luther King, Jr. gave his famous "I Have a Dream" speech in 1963).

UNITED STATES

- Teachers are hired by local school districts.

- Only eleven states have extra funding to support the additional needs of students in high-poverty areas.

- States that spend more on education offer higher teachers' salaries that are comparable with other middle-class professions. Teachers in states with lower funding sometimes need to supplement their income with additional work.

- Richer areas, which collect more money through property taxes, tend to have better schools. Some wealthy students' schools are funded at double the rate of poorer students' schools.

- The U.S. spends more on education than Japan but has vastly different systems and academic outcomes across states and school districts.

- The gaps in educational spending between the lowest- and highest-funded states are growing.

STANDING TOGETHER

We've talked about four major reasons for increasing inequality: automation, globalization, financialization, and under-taxation of the rich.

There's one more reason to explore (and it, too, ends in "-ation"): **unionization.** More specifically, less unionization has made inequality worse—and that's bad news for young people like Ben Trinh who are on the verge of entering the workforce.

In some American states, "right-to-work" laws prevent employers from negotiating with unions that require all employees to be members and pay dues. This prevents employees from being forced to join a union if they'd rather not. But not representing all employees severely undercuts the union's ability to negotiate on behalf of its members. Protests and other actions are most effective when everyone participates.

Unionization is the process of gathering workers into unions—groups that deal with their employers as one. Unions handle negotiations over pay rates, benefits, vacations, scheduling, safety conditions, and more. When negotiations break down, union members may go on strike, refusing to work until the employer offers a better deal.

Wages and working conditions vastly improved for workers after the Industrial Revolution, thanks to the rise of unions. During the manufacturing boom that followed World War II, they helped millions of blue-collar workers join the middle class. But higher wages made it hard to compete with overseas companies that could produce goods for less. So, just like the auto manufacturer in the Trinh family's hometown, corporations began moving their product assembly to foreign countries or investing in automation that eliminated jobs. Corporations also pressured governments to roll back the workers' rights in laws and to pass laws that made it harder for unions to be effective. As a result, unions in the private sector—the part of the economy run by companies and individuals, not government—have lost much of their bargaining power, and union membership has declined since its peak in the early 1950s.

A NEW GIG

Young workers are less likely to join unions than older workers and more likely to work in non-unionized companies and industries, like the hospitality industry, retail stores, and call centers. They're more likely to find themselves in temporary or part-time jobs and are a large part of the gig economy's workforce.

The **gig economy** (or **platform economy**) is made up of "independent contractors"—another way of saying that you run your own business and sign contracts to do work that's often temporary or part-time. This includes "office jobs," such as business consultants, designers, and freelance editors, and working for web- and app-based platforms, such as food-delivery services.

On the surface, there are advantages to working for these platforms. The hours are usually flexible, which means you can fit part-time gigs around full-time employment or classes. This is especially attractive to young people like Ben Trinh, who may need to work while going to school. Gig jobs can also help immigrants, who make up a large part of the gig economy workforce, by boosting their earnings in their adopted country. But the more you depend on gigs for income, the greater the risks. There's no guarantee your gigs will add up to the minimum wage. Your employer doesn't collect taxes and other payroll deductions, so you'll be responsible for filing and paying those yourself. There's no paid time off or benefits, and there may be serious safety concerns, from road hazards to dealing with aggressive passengers. This widens the economic gaps between low-paid independent contractors and the employers who reap all the profits.

These worries have inspired a new wave of organizing on behalf of workers' rights. Food-delivery couriers in Norway and Japan have formed unions to fight for better wages and safety conditions. In the United Kingdom, a union called United Voices of the World, which mostly represents immigrant workers, won pay raises and the right to strike from Uber. Much of this organizing is taking place online, harnessing the power of websites and apps to help workers stand together.

Several of the more equal OECD countries still have relatively high rates of membership in private-sector unions. In Germany, which has a strong manufacturing industry, union representatives sit on company boards to ensure workers' rights and concerns are heard. In Sweden and Australia, wages are fixed across industries through negotiations between companies, the government, and unions.

TAKING CARE OF EACH OTHER

It can be hard enough to climb the economic ladder without one hand tied behind your back—or in a sling.

Injuries, illnesses, and mental health issues can prevent people from working and earning income. In the United States, where millions of people have inadequate private health insurance or no insurance at all, a health crisis can drain a family's savings, sink them into debt, or force them into bankruptcy.

As bad as the financial toll can be on lower- and middle-income families, even worse are the health consequences. The U.S. government spends more per person on health care than any other OECD country—and yet has less to show for it. Americans have a lower life expectancy, higher infant mortality (death rates for babies in their first year), and more people with unmanaged diabetes.

More than half a million Americans declare bankruptcy each year because of medical bills or time off work due to health problems. As many as two-thirds of personal bankruptcies in the U.S. are caused by or connected to medical issues.

In 2020, Canada's federal government signed an agreement with thirty-four First Nations in the province of Manitoba that enabled Indigenous communities to take over the control and design of their health-care services to better suit their needs.

In neighboring Canada, health insurance is run and paid for by the government. Each citizen chips in by paying income tax and sales tax. Those taxes go up or down depending on how much someone earns and how much they spend. However much each taxpayer chips in, they and their families are entitled to the same health care as everyone else.

No health-care system is perfect. Canadians have long complained about the wait times for elective (non-life-threatening) procedures, and the country's health-care system doesn't cover the cost of most prescriptions, dental care, or eye care. But on balance, most universal health-care systems have more pros than cons—for both citizens and governments. For example, they allow governments to negotiate with **pharmaceutical** companies to bring down prices. Most importantly, universal health care means that the quality of treatment you receive doesn't depend on your ability to pay medical bills. Whether you need a single stitch or a new heart, everyone has equal access to care.

Members of the LGBTQ2+ community experience higher rates of anxiety, stress, and depression—about twice that of the non-LGBTQ2+ population. Australia's MindOut Project is a network of organizations that work together and with government on mental-health and suicide-prevention services for LGBTQ2+ people. The services are tailored to the special needs of Indigenous peoples, youth, people with intersex bodies, and people with disabilities.

Accepting Their Share

Why do the rich in some countries willingly pay high taxes to pay for services and the rich in other countries organize against it? One possibility is that those who accept high taxes feel they are part of a community that they should support. They may believe that they benefit, directly or indirectly, when health care, better-quality education, and childcare are available for everyone. And since many of these high earners live in more-equal countries, where policies like government-funded health care have been in place for a long time, history may have shown the value of working together to close economic gaps.

For the rural population of Finland, accessing health care can be challenging, especially for people with disabilities that affect their mobility, and for the elderly. A project called "Mallu Does the Rounds" tested out mobile medical services, outfitting a bus staffed with nurses that toured the South Karelia region. The bus brought health services directly to 100,000 potential patients, providing such services as flu vaccines, removing stitches, and offering health guidance.

BRINGING IT HOME

The last arena in which we will look at the effects of inequality and the efforts to fight it couldn't be closer to home: housing.

With the growth of the financial sector and industries like technology, jobs have become concentrated in cities around the world. All too often, though, the available housing doesn't keep up with a city's rising population, making it more expensive. As a result, lower- and middle-income households spend most of their earnings just keeping a roof over their heads.

Unless you're rich, you may have little to no money left over to build your family's wealth.

So, what's a government to do? As with all things political, it depends on who you ask. Here are just a few of the strategies used by cities around the world that can help increase the available housing—as well as the challenges to getting things done.

- Subsidized housing makes homes more affordable for low-income families, while shelters provide refuge for homeless people and others in need.
- Owners of single-family dwellings may resist the addition of apartments and shelters in their neighborhoods because they could change the neighborhood's character and affect their property values.

- Zoning trade-offs can require developers to add lower-cost housing units to new buildings in exchange for lifting restrictions on a building's height.
- Getting rid of restrictions on development doesn't always guarantee developers will add housing—or if they do, that the housing will be affordable.

A 2019 United Nations report strongly condemned global housing conditions for Indigenous peoples for violating their right to live with security and dignity. Indigenous peoples are more likely to live in unsafe environments, to have their land forcibly taken from them, and to become homeless. The report included guidelines for improving these conditions.

Many of Tokyo's older structures were made of wood, which burns easily, is vulnerable to earthquakes, and degrades over time. Through rebuilding, Tokyo has greatly increased its available housing since 2000, replacing single-family homes with multi-unit buildings and decreasing housing prices in the process.

Projects that pair senior citizens with university students provide seniors with living assistance and companionship in exchange for affordable housing.

CAFE

- New developments contribute to **gentrification**—making a neighborhood more affluent.
- Gentrification can drive up property taxes and living expenses to levels that are unaffordable to long-time residents.

- Increasing public transit makes neighborhoods more livable and improves commuting times.
- Public transit is expensive and may require higher property taxes from families who already feel stretched.

THE TAKEAWAY

Equality doesn't happen by accident. It takes specific policies and programs that work to build a better society for everyone.

What Else We've Learned

 Inequality in education, health care, and housing mirrors other forms of inequality, with members of marginalized communities having less access.

 Unions still have a role to play in ensuring workers receive fair compensation and work in safe environments.

 A good education for all students begins with a system that aims to treat every student equally.

Creating affordable housing requires the cooperation of an entire community to overcome potential roadblocks.

IDEAS IN ACTION

Thousands of young workers are being hired through "zero-hours contracts," which offer no guarantees for how many hours will be worked or how they will be scheduled. These workers may be vulnerable to shady business practices, such as employers keeping tips for themselves or unsafe working conditions. The Scottish campaign BetterThanZero was created to address the increase in this precarious work, particularly among young workers. BetterThanZero informs workers of their rights through monthly meetings, workplace posters, and social media; pressures governments to find ways to protect workers; and partners with other labor organizations to campaign against companies that don't respect workers' rights.

DIGGING DEEPER

You can find out how much funding your school district receives by researching school board budgets and news reports, or contacting your local elected representatives. How does your district compare to others in your region? If there are big differences, should the funding of districts be more equal, and if so, how would you accomplish that?

LEARN MORE!

Indspire
indspire.ca

Asean Johnson
@AseanCJohnson

MindOut
lgbtihealth.org.au/mindout

"Report on the Right to Adequate Housing of Indigenous Peoples" from the UN Office of the High Commissioner for Human Rights
ohchr.org/EN/Issues/Housing/Pages/AdequateHousing Indigenous-Peoples.aspx

BetterThanZero
betterthanzero.scot

CHAPTER 9

Shaping the Future

Introduction:

PART OF THE SOLUTION

Disability activist Mia Ives-Rublee spent much of her childhood and young adulthood learning how to cope with physical challenges, which include using a wheelchair. But she had a transformative experience when she attended the Paralympic Games for the first time. There, she saw athletes competing fiercely and making the most of their abilities. She became an athlete herself, competing in wheelchair track, fencing, and adaptive CrossFit.

She turned her attention to **civil rights**, helping people with mental disabilities get jobs and find community services, and advising activists on how to make protests accessible to everyone. In 2017, she founded the disability caucus of the Women's March on Washington, which saw hundreds of thousands of people across the United States and around the world standing up for women's and human rights. The caucus provided information and resources for marchers with disabilities, enabling more than 41,000 people to participate.

In all OECD countries, speaking out against inequality, injustice, and unfairness is a right—and it can be a privilege. Physical or mental disabilities can create barriers to participating in activism, and those in power may choose to listen to only selected voices.

The kind of action that creates change needs to be inclusive, giving everyone a chance to be seen and heard. It also requires allies. Whether it's straight students supporting LGBTQ2+ students by joining a gay-straight alliance at school, white protesters stepping between Black protesters and police during Black Lives Matter marches, or richer people promoting tax policies that benefit poorer people—if we want a more equal society, we've got to join hands up and down the ladder.

In this final chapter, we offer a quick primer for getting involved in causes related to inequality. We'll look at successful youth-led movements that can provide inspiration, as well as lessons to be learned from their successes and short-comings. We'll outline the first steps toward becoming politically active and provide resources to help you develop a more detailed plan of action. And we're going to finish making our case for why you can and should tackle inequality to build a more equal, fairer society for all.

PICKING YOUR BATTLES

In 2011, a scrappy group of young protesters camped out in Zuccotti Park in New York City's financial district.

They were protesting social and economic inequality and how big corporations (like those represented on NYC's Wall Street) hurt democracy by taking too much power out of the hands of ordinary workers and voters. "Occupy" grew into an international movement, with protests taking place in nearly a thousand cities in dozens of countries. Its most famous slogan was "We are the 99 percent"—that is, the 99 percent of the population who must stand up to the privileged one percent.

Within months, though, "Occupy" began to fizzle out. Critics have said that its concerns were too broad, that it lacked leadership and solutions. But the movement started a conversation that continues today—about who holds power and how to take it back. That conversation led to the growth of the **progressive** wing of the Democratic Party in the United States, led by Bernie Sanders's campaigns to be the presidential nominee for the party. It helped light a spark of youth activism around climate change, gun control, and other issues important to young people, which continues around the globe.

Inspiring Reads to Help You Get Your Protest On

Know Your Rights and Claim Them: A Guide for Youth, written by Amnesty International, Angelina Jolie, and Geraldine Van Bueren (Zest Books, 2021)

Nevertheless, We Persisted: 48 Voices of Defiance, Strength, and Courage, foreword by Amy Klobuchar (Knopf Books for Young Readers, 2018)

Steal This Country: A Handbook for Resistance, Persistence, and Fixing Almost Everything, written by Alexandra Styron (Viking Books for Young Readers, 2018)

CHOOSING A CAUSE

Some say that "Occupy" didn't fizzle so much as dissolve into many separate campaigns related to equality and democracy. Within the pages of this book, we've seen how inequality is really a collection of issues that affect just about every aspect of your life, from health to housing to hope. All of these issues have a measurable, often negative impact on people's lives—which will only get better if politicians, the people who elect them, and activists stand up for equality.

In the "Digging Deeper" section on page 55, we asked what you think is the fairest way to slice a cake. According to need? According to each person's contribution? In a sense, you could ask the same questions when choosing a cause to support. Where do you see the greatest need? What skills or knowledge do you have to contribute and where can they make the most difference? Which issue is nearest and dearest to your own heart?

Whatever your age or circumstances, you can focus your efforts on the issues that are most important to you and help create real change.

What About Charities?

Working with non-profit organizations and charities can be a great way to learn more about issues related to inequality and connect with like-minded people. But beware of a common argument among rich donors that they shouldn't have to pay their fair share in taxes because they give so much money away. Charity is no substitute for equality-promoting public goods provided by government.

To be sure, wealthy people have done a lot of good through generous donations. The Bill and Melinda Gates Foundation alone has given a whopping $60 billion USD to help improve the health of the globe's poorest people. There are dangers, though, in relying too much on charity to solve a society's problems. First, charity is voluntary—no one is compelled to help out. Counting on charity means handing over to rich citizens the power to determine which causes are most important and how to address them. It means letting the people on top make all the decisions instead of those who need the help. Since inequality affects everyone in a society, everyone should have a chance to influence those decisions through their elected representatives.

DOES YOUTH ACTION WORK?

**If inequality has political causes,
then politics must be part of the solution.**

That means electing politicians and political parties that see inequality as a problem and are willing to address it as a priority. But politics don't begin and end at the ballot box, and you don't have to be old enough to vote to be the pressure that influences political outcomes.

After the 2018 mass shooting at Marjory Stoneman Douglas High School in Parkland, Florida, young survivors started the March for Our Lives national campaign to advocate for stronger gun control laws. A month later, a million protesters across the country took to the streets to demand change. More than 200 regional chapters have now opened across the country, and one of their main activities is registering first-time voters and encouraging them to vote.

Did it help? Gun control was a significant issue in the 2018 midterm elections for the U.S. Congress and state governors' races, with more candidates taking a strong stance on the need for stricter gun laws than in previous elections.

The election also saw a 10 percent increase in young voter turnout—which some have credited to the rise of youth activism, including March for Our Lives. As importantly, it sent a clear message that gun control could become an even bigger issue in future elections when more young activists become old enough to vote.

Youth protestors have also taken on smaller fights with big impacts. While March for Our Lives was expanding its mission to mobilize young voters and activists, teens in New Jersey were lobbying the state government to include young workers in a proposed increase to the minimum wage. The original bill stated that adult workers would reach $15 per hour by 2024, but teens under eighteen wouldn't reach the $15 mark until 2029. The five-year time gap for teen workers was scrapped.

You see, when people raise their voices loudly enough, whether about gun control or problems that lead to economic inequality, those in power have to listen—even if those voices are young.

🌐 Youth Activist Toolkit, Advocates for Youth *advocatesforyouth.org/ resources/curriula-education/ youth-activist-toolkit*

🌐 "How to Strengthen Your Message with Data," Voices of Youth, UNICEF's digital community for youth by youth *voicesofyouth.org/act/ how-strengthen- your-message-data*

🌐 "The E-manual on E-activism," SALTO-YOUTH (Support, Advanced Learning and Training Opportunities for Youth) *toolbox.salto-youth.net/2014*

A Quick-Start Guide to Making Protests More Accessible

- Invite people with disabilities to serve on your planning committee.
- Remember that not all disabilities are visible or obvious. Illness, chronic pain, and mental health issues can also create barriers to participation.
- Create an e-campaign for people who cannot attend in person. Examples are live and/or recorded video coverage of speeches and marches, as well as ways to partici- pate through social media.
- Ensure your protest area has a gathering place for those with limited mobility.
- Indoor spaces should have ramps, wide doorways, accessible wash- rooms, and adequate spaces for wheelchairs and other mobility devices.
- Hire a sign-language interpreter for public speeches and announcements.
- Include alt-text to describe images used in social media and on websites, for the visually impaired.
- Have volunteers on hand to help those who are in need of extra assistance.

GETTING POLITICAL

(When you're too young to vote.)

Politicians who want to address inequality can face opposition from all corners: lobbyists, special interest groups, corporations, other political parties, and even members of their own party! They have a much better chance of getting things done when they are backed by large, well-informed, noisy political movements. That includes youth-led campaigns, as well as individuals like you who want to be part of meaningful change.

Here are a few ways you can get involved with elections and elected representatives in your area—at the local, regional, or national level.

LEARN ABOUT YOUR ELECTED REPRESENTATIVES

Most elected representatives have websites that outline the issues they campaigned on, and many governments publish online records that show how politicians voted on bills, budgets, and proposed policies. Are they taking action to reduce inequality?

BE IN TOUCH

Call or write to your elected representatives to express your concerns or attend events where they interact with voters, such as a town hall meeting. Politicians really do take note of what issues stir up their constituents, so be persistent!

LOOK FOR EQUALITY-PROMOTING PLATFORMS

When a local, state, or federal election rolls around, get informed about each candidate's platform—the goals they are promising to pursue if they are elected. Are they enthusiastic supporters of public goods and fair taxes? Where do they stand on issues of particular interest to young voters, like the high cost of post-secondary tuition, minimum wage, and climate change?

BOOST YOUR FAVORITES

Promote politicians and political parties who share your values. You can hold a fundraiser for their next election campaign, volunteer to go door to door to spread the word about candidates you endorse, ask your parents to put a sign on your lawn or in a window, or express your enthusiasm through social media.

In 2018, the Canadian government announced the formation of the Prime Minister's Youth Council, which advises the prime minister directly on issues of particular interest to young Canadians.

GET OUT THE VOTE

Support organizations that promote voting and remove obstacles to voting. You could work with a group that helps people register to vote, share information about how to vote, or fundraise to pay for legal action to protect voting rights.

SHARE YOUR KNOWLEDGE

Youth advisory councils provide opportunities to talk to decision-makers about issues that are important to you. They guide the policies of public libraries, hospitals, non-profits, city councils, and more. Contact your local councils to find out how to join—or talk to your elected representatives about how to start one.

EMBRACE INTERSECTIONALITY

Different aspects of our identities—gender, ethnicity, sexual orientation, ability, etc.–can intersect, or overlap. **"Intersectionality"**, a term coined by Kimberlé Crenshaw, means acknowledging how these overlapping identities may cause people to suffer multiple disadvantages at the same time. The more we understand about how intersectionality shapes a person's experiences, the more inclusive we can be with the action we take. For example, a campaign to improve services for people with disabilities should consider how someone who has a disability and is a member of another marginalized community may face extra barriers to accessing those services.

THE TAKEAWAY

With a righteous cause, a solid plan, and the right tools, you can take on inequality before you're old enough to vote.

What Else We've Learned

 Inequality can be tackled as an overarching issue or related issues.

 Young voices have the power to provoke meaningful change.

 Supporting your local elected representatives or their challengers is a great way to get involved in politics.

IDEAS IN ACTION

The Debt Collective is a unique union formed not by workers but by people in debt, including those with sizable student loans. Members work together to dispute the terms of their loans, pressure politicians to take action against unfair and harmful loan policies, and even go on strike—refusing to repay loans—to push for change.

DIGGING DEEPER

In many OECD countries, young people vote in much smaller numbers than older voters. One proposal to address this issue is bringing the voting age down to as low as sixteen, but will teen voters turn out? Research indicates that younger voters are more likely to participate when the process is easier or more straightforward, like being automatically registered to vote or having a mail-in voting option. But it also appears there are big differences in enthusiasm for voting among young people in different countries. Why do you think it's so hard to coax young voters to the polls and what can be done about it?

LEARN MORE!

Mia Ives-Rublee
@seemiaroll

Disability March
disabilitymarch.com

March For Our Lives
marchforourlives.com

Debt Collective
debtcollective.org

THE PLAYLIST

"Fight the Power"—Public Enemy

"For What It's Worth"—Buffalo Springfield

"Formation"—Beyoncé

"Get Up, Stand Up"—Bob Marley and the Wailers

"Mercy"—Miko Marks & the Resurrectors

"Quiet"—MILCK

Conclusion

Over the course of this book, we've touched on many issues and ideas related to economic inequality and its connections to other forms of inequality. You may find yourself wanting to know more about some of these subjects—and that's great! There is so much to question and learn and explore.

We hope we've given you the information and understanding you need to begin thinking about how you can help make the world a more equal place and that you will investigate the additional resources highlighted throughout the book. And we hope that if anyone ever asks what *you* think about economic inequality, you'll be ready with these takeaway truths.

Inequality . . .

affects everybody

has multiple causes

MATTERS

can and should be reduced

requires political solutions

is made up of smaller issues
that can be tackled individually

needs young people like you to rally
behind the cause in order to secure their future
and ensure no one gets left behind.

GLOSSARY

Wherever possible, we have defined terms on the pages where they are used. The following terms may require additional explanation.

biodiversity
The diversity, or variety, of forms of life on Earth

bonds
A loan made by an investor to a company or government that is paid back on a particular date with interest

capital gains
The profit earned on the sale of an asset when the selling price is higher than the original purchase price

cisgender
Refers to a person whose gender identity matches the gender they were assigned at birth

civil rights
The rights of all citizens to equal opportunity and equal treatment under the law

class action suit
A legal action filed by a group of people against a single defendant accused of causing them harm

gender
The broad social traits of women, men, boys, girls, and gender-diverse people, including attributes, behavior, roles, and forms of expression. Gender may be nonbinary, meaning not one or the other (e.g., male or female). It may be nonconforming: not conforming to traditional ideas about gender

incorporated
A legal process that turns a company into a corporation, which gives it particular rights under the law

insurance
An agreement to cover potential financial costs due to damage, loss, illness, or death in exchange for the payment of premiums (regular payments)

interest
Extra money charged on a loan, usually a percentage of the amount originally borrowed

investments
Assets purchased in order to gain profit or another financial advantage and build wealth

investors
People or organizations that purchase, or invest in, assets in order to earn a profit or gain another financial advantage

loan

A sum of money borrowed, often repaid with interest

monetary policies

A country's central bank's planned actions to control the supply of money and its value

parliament

A type of legislature, or body of government, made up of representatives elected by voters, which represents their interests, makes laws, and oversees government actions

per capita

A way of saying "per person" or "for each person" in order to compare a figure to the size of a population

pharmaceutical

Relating to drugs made by drug companies

progressive

A person or organization that believes in and promotes continued improvements to society, including through government actions

resources

1. Sources of support or assistance
2. Supply of money for spending, or assets that can be sold for cash
3. Things found in nature that are useful to humans

stocks

The partial ownership in one or more companies by buying a collection of shares. Sometimes used interchangeably with "shares," but a share is a single unit of ownership (see page 53)

tax credits

An amount of money that may be subtracted from taxes owed to the government

transgender

Refers to a person who has transitioned to a different gender identity than the one assigned to them at birth

trust accounts

A financial account in which funds are held for the future benefit of one person, but managed at the present time by another person on their behalf

In the early twentieth century, the term "white-collar" workers came to mean those who wear suit-shirts with turned-down collars on the job. The first mention of blue-collar workers may have appeared in the *Times* newspaper of Alden, Iowa, in 1924: "If we may call professions and office positions white collar jobs, we may call the trades blue collar jobs." By "the trades," the newspaper meant jobs outside of office settings, such as electricians and construction workers. These jobs require hands-on skills training but lower levels of formal education.

INDEX

Note: Page numbers in *italics* refer to illustrations.